W9-AQS-587

BY THE EDITORS OF CONSUMER GUIDE®

MINIATURES

BEEKMAN HOUSE

NEW YORK

Contents

Manufactured in the United States of America
1 2 3 4 5 6 7 8 9 10

Library of Congress Catalog Card Number: 79-88916
ISBN: 0-517-298953

This edition published by
Beekman House
A Division of Crown Publishers, Inc.
One Park Avenue
New York, N.Y. 10016

Photo Credits: Bill Miller; Carlson's Miniatures, Inc., Delevan, WI; Cir-Kit Concepts, Inc., Rochester, MN; Color West Ltd., Broadview, IL; Doreen Sinnett Designs, Inc., Newport Beach, CA; The Enchanted Dollhouse, Manchester Center, VT; Robin's Roost, Grayslake, IL; Scientific Models, Berkeley Heights, NJ; Smithsonian Institution, Washington, D.C.

Illustrations: Steven Boswick

1

Introduction

IF YOU SHOULD VISIT the Museum of History and Technology at the Smithsonian Institution in Washington, D.C., and take a particular escalator to its upper floors, you would see an unusual sight—the Faith Bradford dollhouse, an imposing 22-room dollhouse built in the early 1900s. The crowds that gather around it day after day are almost as remarkable as the dollhouse itself and serve as a powerful testimony to the fascination that miniatures hold for just about everyone.

The eye, the mind and the imagination have always been enchanted by miniatures, but never before has the appreciation of small and perfect things been so widespread as within the last decade. Since the early 1970s, thousands of Americans have become caught up in the creation and collection of miniaturized houses, furnishings and accessories. The eye seems to find endless delight in contemplating tiny things. For the mind, there is a challenge in the very idea of miniaturization. It has played a special role in our time. As the horizons of our technology expand to the point where even the planets are within our reach, the tools of our accomplishments become smaller and smaller. A man can hold in his two hands a tiny computer that can help him to conquer space. "Miniature" may mean small, but definitely not insignificant.

Our sense of fun and fantasy are stimulated by miniatures. There are few activities in which we are so free to recreate a historical period, fulfill a dream, express personal interest and tastes or tell a story. The world of miniatures is the reconstruction on a small scale of our big, "real" world, but with an important difference: this is a world that we create for ourselves. We are free to include or exclude whatever we wish.

2

3

Some of the best scale pieces available in miniature are: a Chippendale chair by Harry Cooke; violin by W. Foster Tracy; kneehole desk by Paul Runyon; and stool with petit point upholstery by Virginia Merrill. From left to right on the desk is an Imari bowl by Deborah McKnight, an inkstand by Eugene Kupjack and a tea caddy by Wm. Robertson. The handblown glass is by Francis Whittemore (1). The Faith Bradford house, with its 22 rooms, is surely one to "get lost" in (2). Colleen Moore's Castle offers residence to the fantasies of children and adults alike (3).

We can cross barriers of time and space, and we need not consider the practicalities that continually limit us in the "big" world. It is a world where the imagination can bring to reality a perfection never realized full-size.

This new tide of enthusiasm over miniatures has produced a multitude of shops catering to miniature collectors and craftspeople all over the nation. A host of books and new magazines devoted to the subject have been published just within the past four years. Manufacturers have begun to produce an abundance of kits, finished items and craft materials, all aimed at a new kind of consumer, the miniaturist. And everywhere, during the fall and spring months, there are miniature shows—fairs where the public comes in droves to see and to buy the tiny wares displayed by miniatures craftspeople and dealers.

The purpose of *Miniatures* is to act as a guide in the land of Lilliput. As in Gulliver's kingdom, the objects may be miniscule, but the world they represent is as vast and diverse as the imagination.

How Big is Small?

There are many kinds of miniature hobbies, such as model railroading, model airplanes and military miniatures. However, it is generally acknowledged that the collective term "miniatures" refers to the reproduction of small-scale items representative of everyday, domestic life. The miniaturist attempts to capture in exact detail a time, a place and an atmosphere. The illusion is achieved through scale, the critical factor in precision miniature work.

Scale is simply the relationship of a miniature to its full-size counterpart. In all miniature or model work, adherence to scale in every aspect of reproduction determines how realistic the miniature will appear to the observer. The most widely used scale in the miniatures hobby is one inch equals one foot, or one-twelfth scale. This simply means that everything in a miniature room or setting must be one-twelfth full size. This is an especially easy scale to use. The miniaturist need only read inches for feet to determine the dimensions. Thus, a room measuring eight and a half by twelve feet in full size would measure eight and a half by twelve inches (one foot) in miniature. A six-foot tall china cabinet would be reduced to six inches tall, a five-foot long table would be five inches long, and so forth. When working with smaller dimensions, of course, it becomes a little more complicated, but just keep dividing by twelve. A calculator is helpful, and there are special conversion rulers on the market, but it all becomes easier with practice and, in time, the eye itself becomes skilled in judging scale.

The important thing is that everything in a miniature setting be to scale. If even one item is out of proportion, the illusion of reality is spoiled. For example, a chest of drawers may be built perfectly to scale, but if its drawer pulls are too large, the effect is lost. A perfect miniature is one which is so lifelike that, if you saw a photograph of it, you would be unable to tell whether or not it was a miniature. It's not an impossible goal. It has been achieved many times by many miniaturists.

Undoubtedly, the most famous example of impeccable miniatures is the Thorne Rooms at the Art Institute of Chicago. These 68 rooms were conceived, planned and commissioned by Mrs. James Ward Thorne during the 1920s for the purpose of providing a history of American and European interiors. The finest miniatures craftspeople of the time were engaged to work on the rooms, with the result that they are so flawlessly executed, with such faithful adherence to scale, that they are the recognized epitome of miniature work.

The Thorne Rooms not only serve to illustrate the heights of artistry and craftsmanship that can be reached, but they also prove that miniatures are not toys, in spite of the associations that the word "dollhouse" may have for many people. Dollhouses are children's playthings. Add miniatures, and they become adult diversion.

The very first dollhouse on record is one commissioned by Albrecht V, Duke of Bavaria, in 1558 for his young daughter. Although originally intended to be a toy, it wound up as part of the Duke's art collection, becoming the first of a long line of dollhouses initially begun for children, but ultimately confiscated by the adult world.

Miniatures captured the imaginations of well-to-do Dutch merchants of the 17th and 18th centuries who spent fortunes on detailed cabinets of miniature rooms, many of which can now be seen in Amsterdam's Rijksmuseum. In England in the 18th century, "babies' houses" were "in," but in spite of their name they were intended for adults, not children. Like the Dutch cabinets, these contained the very finest craftsmanship—brocades, tapestries, porcelain, sterling silver and Chippendale furniture made by the man himself.

1

Regardless of their magnificence, these early miniatures had flaws that modern miniaturists would find intolerable. Scale was often disregarded, and the dollhouses frequently contained architectural blunders (i.e. stairways leading to nowhere) that limited the illusion of realism. Still, these expensive and elaborate miniature settings began a trend among the leisured class which continues today.

The Ultimate Dollhouse

Probably the ultimate dollhouse is the one built in 1924 for Queen Mary of England by her loyal subjects. It is

2

The Colleen Moore Castle contains a chapel which suggests the riches of a religious empire but was built with the wealth, love and fantasy of a Hollywood star for all to enjoy (1). In the drawing room a diamond, emerald and pearl chandelier hangs from a ceiling painted with clouds. The story of Cinderella is depicted in the murals on the walls (2).

without question the most famous dollhouse in the world. Built over a period of four years, it is a testimony to the devotion of those people who pooled their talents and resources, adding detail after detail so that the completed house is a treasury of finely wrought artifacts. The wine cellar contains bottles of real wine and other alcoholic beverages, a fact which caused some disturbance and vocal objections among Prohibitionists of the time. The books lining the shelves of the library are all handwritten, original manuscripts by leading British authors. Even the plumbing and the elevators work! The Queen Mary dollhouse, reflecting as it does the talent and effort of an entire nation, has served to lift miniatures cut of the realm of playthings.

On this side of the Atlantic, there are many fine old dollhouses, kept in museums or other public places (see "Sources" at the end of this book), which were originally built as toys, as models of existing buildings or as works of art for adult pleasure. The best known American dollhouse is Colleen Moore's Castle, commissioned by the movie star and miniatures enthusiast in 1935. No effort or expense was spared in its creation and furnishing, which delight both miniatures connoisseurs and children. It is a flight of fancy that brings to life the characters and events of children's literature. King Arthur, The Wizard of Oz, Aladdin, Cinderella and other fairy tale figures are represented throughout the house. But it is a fantasy within the confines of scale and demanding craftsmanship. After its completion, the castle toured the country, drawing crowds of thousands wherever it was exhibited. Today, it is on display at Chicago's Museum of Science and Industry.

1

The Scope Of Miniatures

YOU CAN ENJOY the world of miniatures in one of several ways. The particular way you choose will depend upon your tastes and interests and the kind of person you are. If you're the imaginative type, you will approach the hobby differently from one who is exacting and practical. Fortunately, in miniatures, there is room for all.

Miniatures are also an ideal family hobby. They encompass so many different skills and interests that, regardless of age, sex or ability, everyone can take part in the construction and decoration of a dollhouse.

Your budget will also be an important factor in determining how you become involved in the hobby. It is possible to spend enormous amounts of money on miniatures. There are individual miniature collections worth thousands of dollars, and there are craftspeople whose work commands extremely high prices ($1,500 for a secretary desk; $10,000 for a custom-built unfurnished house). At this level, miniatures become more an investment than a hobby.

But satisfaction can be derived as much from time and effort spent as from money invested. If you choose to approach miniatures primarily as a collector, it is inevitable that you will spend money. On the other hand, if your talents and interests lie more in the area of crafts, you can accomplish a lot at relatively little cost. Most miniaturists take a middle road, crafting those items that they are able to make and enjoy making, and filling in with manufactured or others' handcrafted pieces. Both crafters and collectors can find an expression of some facet of themselves. There are few hobbies that offer so many possibilities to so many different kinds of people.

Historical Reproductions

One approach to miniatures is to use them as a vehicle for capturing the details and, hence, the

2

3

This ultra-modern glass, wood, stucco and stone house provides unlimited opportunity for creative decorating (1). Victorian doll-houses, designed with subtle, good-taste gingerbread, reflect the time of trollies and big Sunday suppers (2). A dollhouse can be customized using a variety of outside treat-ments--suitably selected (3).

atmosphere of earlier historical periods. History buffs, or anyone who has dreamed of living in another time, find this type of miniature work especially enjoyable.

Since the upsurge of interest in miniatures coincided with the American Bicentennial, many people entered into the hobby by the historical route. In a year when national attention was focused on the Revolutionary period, to reproduce the homes and public buildings of that time seemed only natural. Many painlessly studied history while doing research for a miniature room. Through canopy beds, fire screens, spinning wheels, candlesticks and many other details of early America, the Revolutionary period came to life.

History has always dominated the miniatures hobby in that the majority of people involved reproduce homes, rooms, furniture and accessories of the past rather than contemporary styles. Considerable research is required to faithfully reproduce the furniture and accessories of the period selected. The worst gaffe a historical miniaturist can make is anachronism, or placing the items out of their proper time sequence. For instance, you should never place an early 20th century wall telephone, however quaint its appearance, in a late 19th century parlor!

Avoiding an error is not always easy. Details such as lighting (oil lamps, candles, gaslights, etc.), cooking utensils and furniture styles can quickly betray faulty historical knowledge. But for the miniaturist on this path, part of the fun is in tracking down the facts that will make the setting accurate.

Like every facet of miniatures, the historical approach provides its own challenges and satisfactions. Because of its emphasis on the factual rather than on fantasy, it is probably the most demanding. Authenticity is the ultimate goal. Every miniature piece created has a prototype in history; everything must properly represent its period in time. There are purists who go to extremes, but as a beginner who is attracted

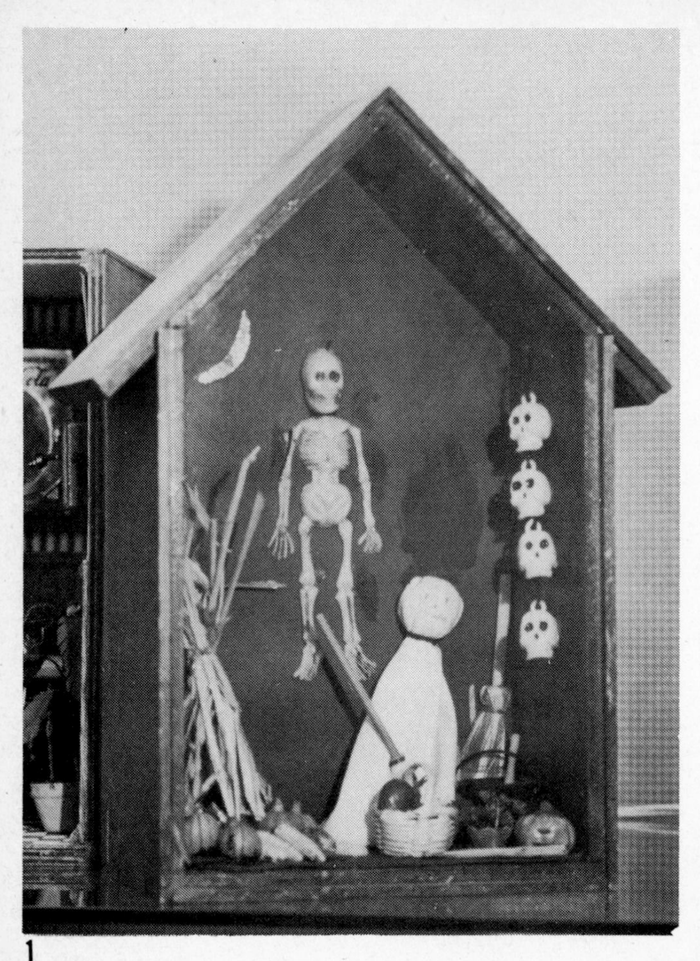

1

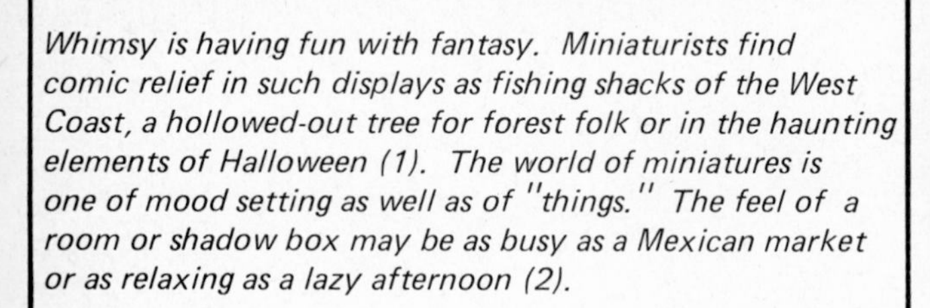

Whimsy is having fun with fantasy. Miniaturists find comic relief in such displays as fishing shacks of the West Coast, a hollowed-out tree for forest folk or in the haunting elements of Halloween (1). The world of miniatures is one of mood setting as well as of "things." The feel of a room or shadow box may be as busy as a Mexican market or as relaxing as a lazy afternoon (2).

2

by this approach, don't be discouraged. It is entirely possible to create historically accurate settings without becoming a fanatic to detail.

Nostalgia

The general store, circa 1900, is an old nostalgia standby with its brightly colored bolts of yard goods piled on the shelves behind the counter, its cheery potbellied stove, its post office boxes and its jars of penny candy. Other miniature favorites are Grandmother's Kitchen, the Little Red Schoolhouse and the Old Farmstead. Like the historians, the "old timers" attempt to reproduce a past era. However, their emphasis is on the flavor of a time and the warm feelings associated with it rather than on exact duplication of specific buildings and pieces of furniture. They, too, have no tolerance for faulty time frames, but their sources are not historical records so much as their own childhood memories and the stories told by their parents and grandparents. In this regard, nostalgic miniatures are often very personal and meaningful.

Efforts are usually made in this miniatures area to suggest human activity in a setting. If dolls are not used (and very often they are not), the inhabitants are hinted at with a book and spectacles lying on a chair, slippers under the bed, a loaf of bread just taken from the oven or in other clever ways.

A delightful clutter frequently characterizes these settings, enhancing their homeyness. For this reason,

3

4

"Sunnywood Farm" recaptures the feelings of childhood summers spent visiting grandparents in the country. Inside might be the quaint accessories typical of the time -- braided rugs, potbellied stoves and an upright piano in the parlor. The possibilities for outside embellishments -- chickens in the yard and a tire swing -- are also fun to think about (3). Down the "road" from Sunnywood Farm is the one-room schoolhouse where time ticked by on a big wall clock. At recess, all would flee to the dusty yard for games of jump rope, leap-frog or stickball (4). Every nostalgic detail is important to carry the theme and "feel" of the times represented.

1

nostalgia is often used by the eclectic miniature collector to display his collection. The general store, for instance, provides an opportunity to place under one tiny roof any number of unrelated items. And the more one adds, the more charming it becomes.

Fantasy

Imagination is given free rein in the third approach to miniatures. The possibilities presented by fantasy are limitless indeed.

Colleen Moore's Castle is a prime example of childhood fantasy in miniature, but adult literature also lends itself to miniaturization. Not only do favorite classics like Sherlock Holmes and the works of Charles Dickens repeatedly serve as inspiration for small settings and houses, but even such popular present day fiction as *Star Wars* has been interpreted in miniature. This kind of miniaturization is a sort of three-dimensional literary illustration. The miniaturist is limited by the subject selected and must be faithful to the period in which the work is set. So, historical research can also be required for literary illustration.

Wish fulfillment is another form of miniature fantasy that is probably the most widely used of all. Miniatures provide an untroubled and orderly existence, a healthy escape from the problems of the real world. Because everything is small, everything is manageable, and the hobbyist need include only those things which give pleasure.

Miniatures are also a way to realize an impossible, impractical dream. You might admire large, rambling Victorian houses with their gingerbread, nooks and crannies, and all the charm reminiscent of a more gracious era. On the other hand, consider the maintenance and a life surrounded by massive furniture and dust-collectiong bric-a-brac! A Victorian dollhouse, or even a single room, provides the opportunity to indulge your taste for the era without suffering its handicaps. And, of course, this applies to any architectural or interior style or period.

Anything is possible in miniature. Collectors or craftspeople who specialize in one kind of item (i.e., ceramics, silver, glass, etc.) can use their imaginations to create settings that are perfect foils for their collections. An artist who paints miniature paintings might create an artist's studio or gallery in which to hang them. Someone who makes or collects tiny plants and flowers could house them in a miniature greenhouse. And the possibilities for specialty shops are endless: book stores, millinery shops, bakeries, grocery stores, pottery shops, toy stores.

Sometimes, capricious imagination can lead down a byroad called Whimsy. Perhaps whimsical miniatures can best be understood through a description of a favorite subject, the Mouse House. In the Mouse House, a family of full-size (but not real) mice enjoy the comforts of scale-model furniture and conveniences. Their house is furnished in a simple, rustic style featuring such homey touches as braided rugs and calico curtains. From the quilt-covered beds the mice sleep in, to the wood-burning stove they cook on, the

2

3

A remember-when room, decorated as an old-fashioned soda fountain, can tickle memories of nickel phosphates and penny candy (1). An unfinished door with "stained glass" transom is only one way to enter the world of miniatures (2). A miniature dressmaker's shop would be a unique gift for one who sews (3).

details of the Mouse House reveal all the human-like activities of its inhabitants.

Mouse houses, bear barrels, gnome homes and other such whimsical constructions represent the other extreme from meticulously researched historical reproductions. Between these two are hundreds of ways in which miniatures can be explored. Each one is fun, challenging and rewarding.

Starting Small

The world of miniatures is so diverse it is sometimes difficult for the beginner to know exactly where to begin. No starting point is exactly right for everyone; rather, it is a question of determining the means of entry into miniatures that is most in keeping with your tastes, abilities and budget. Are you fond of ceramics? Perhaps you should begin a miniature ceramics collection which might ultimately be displayed in a miniature pottery shop. Are you fascinated by the domestic life of the Revolutionary period? For you, a small eighteenth century house, or perhaps a single room might be especially satisfying. Are your tastes eclectic? You might consider starting with a fairly large dollhouse which you can furnish as you accumulate various pieces.

Whichever approach you feel drawn to, it is best to familiarize yourself with the hobby before buying anything. First, locate the miniature shows in your area by referring to one of the miniatures publications, all of which carry a calendar of events. A nearby miniatures or craft shop can probably be of help. Next, attend a show and see firsthand some of the fine current work. This is an opportunity to develop your discrimination and establish your own preferences. But be forewarned. You may feel somewhat overwhelmed by the huge selection and the wide range of prices.

As you browse through a show, pick up some catalogs to look through at your leisure. (Many show exhibitors also deal in mail-order and will sell catalogs at their booths.) To cover printing, handling and mailing costs most mail-order houses must charge for their books. This means that an extensive catalog library may represent a substantial outlay of money, but we do recommend that you buy as many as you can afford. This will provide you with an overview of all that is available. (See "Sources" for mail-order houses.)

Finally, be informed about your new hobby by reading as much about it as you possibly can. In addition to several miniatures magazines, there are many books recently published covering such subjects as dollhouse construction and miniatures collecting and construction. The list at the end of *Miniatures* will serve as a guide to those books which we consider most valuable.

Having visited shows, read some magazines and books and acquired a few mail-order catalogs, you should now have a feel for your new hobby. Whether you have decided to become a collector, to make your own furniture and accessories, to develop a miniature room or complete a dollhouse, you've taken the first step into a land of enchantment.

Making Your Own Miniatures

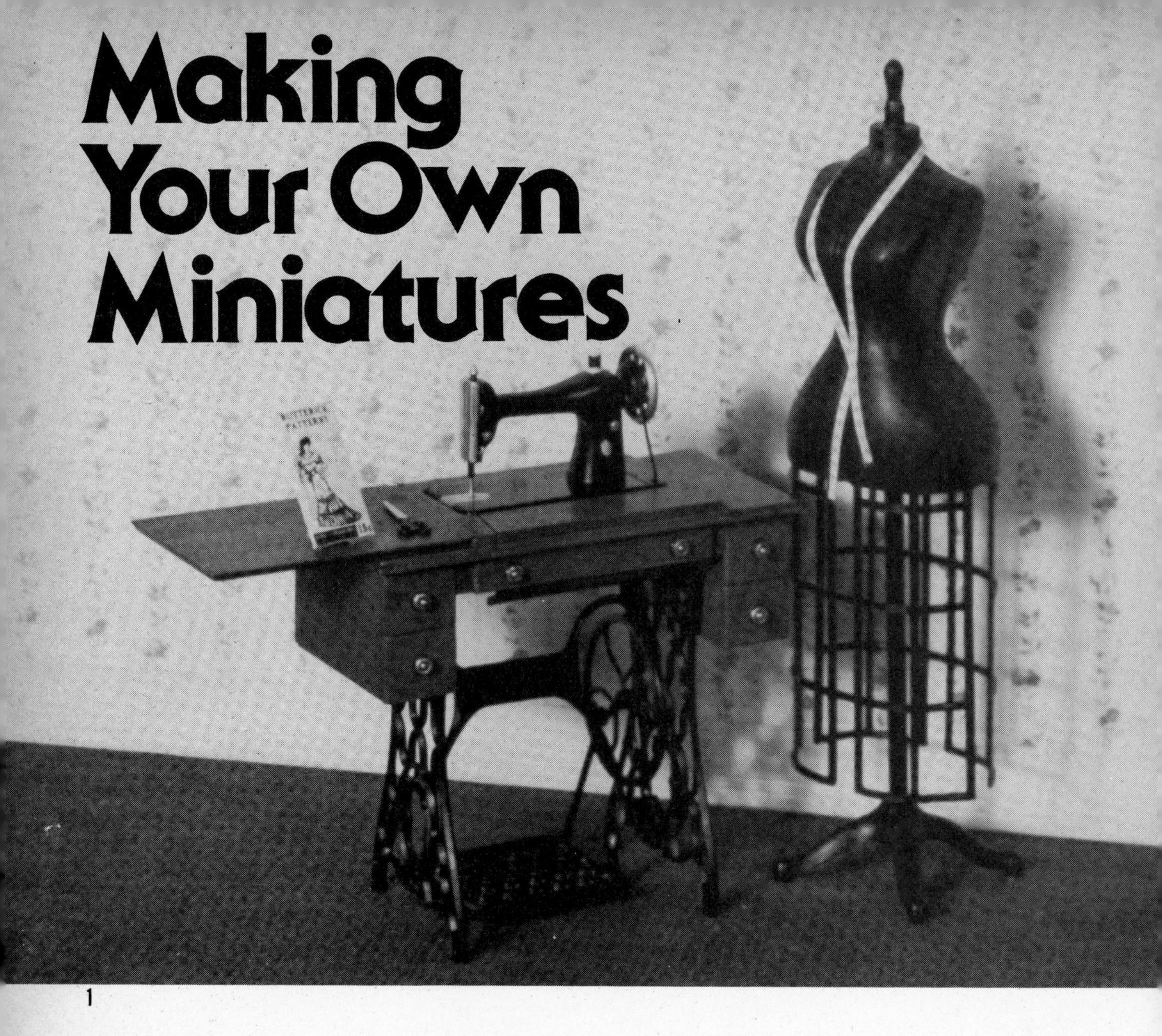

1

EVEN IF YOU'VE DECIDED to concentrate on collecting rather than making miniatures, chances are you'll find yourself doing some kind of hobby-related handwork. To display your collection you'll need a setting, and before long you'll be papering and painting, transforming a box into a fully decorated room.

The majority of miniatures collectors who turn to handcrafts do so to complete collections, either because certain items are impossible to locate or are beyond the budget. For others, however, crafts are what miniatures are all about. To furnish and accessorize a room or dollhouse exclusively with items you have made yourself is a real pleasure.

Miniature making can be easy. It can be begun with the simplest of tools and materials and in minimal working space. Skills develop rapidly; some of the finest contemporary miniature craftspeople have been making miniatures for only a short time.

Furniture Kits

There are several lines of excellent kits now on the market, all to scale and well designed and just right for the novice miniaturist. Making miniature furniture from kits is more economical than buying finished furniture, and you'll be able to acquire a number of pieces at relatively low cost. Assembling a kit also provides practice in gluing, sanding and finishing, all of which will prove helpful if you move on to constructing miniature furniture from scratch.

There are four types of furniture kits available. All four are widely distributed and can be found in miniature, hobby or craft shops, and even in some department, toy and novelty stores. And like most miniatures, they are also carried by many mail order companies. One line includes pre-cut basswood parts, foam and fabric upholstery, glue, hardware and the materials required for finishing the pieces—brush,

2

3

Far from being second-rate, plastics make fine miniatures. This treadle sewing machine and dressmaker's dummy are good examples of quality in modern materials (1). This Colonial secretary exemplifies how well-crafted are miniatures kits (2). Plush and doily-draped, tiny Chippendale chairs are made of hardwood and are available in kit form (3).

sandpaper, stain, etc. (Basswood is light and fragile, so take care in assembling these kits.) Each kit, priced at around $15.00, contains the furnishings for a full room. The line includes a Colonial dining room, living room, modern and old time kitchen, 1930s bathroom, general store, music room, formal hall and nursery. When stained and fully assembled, the furniture is realistic and attractive and offers an excellent nucleus for the development of a dollhouse or miniature room.

Another type of miniature furniture kit provides individually packaged furniture pieces consisting of pre-cut hardwood parts, brass hardware and/or upholstery materials. The two major manufacturers of these kits have based their designs upon actual pieces, so the miniatures produced from the kits are authentic reproductions. The hardwoods of the pre-cut pieces have been carefully selected so even the grain is to scale. All parts are machined to fit together well, enabling even the beginning hobbyist to turn out a perfectly scaled model. The challenge lies in sanding and finishing. By applying some extra effort it's possible to achieve professional-looking results.

Besides the wood furniture kits, there are also lines in plastic and metal. Although these non-authentic materials are scorned by some miniaturists, the finished furniture is amazingly realistic when the basic material has been painted or stained. And because the parts are molded, details such as "carving" and cabriole legs can be incorporated. The manufacturers have capitalized upon this characteristic by specializing in kits in the Queen Anne and Victorian styles, both of which are quite difficult to reproduce in wood. The plastic line in particular is an extensive one, including such offbeat items as an old-fashioned sewing machine and dress form, a Victorian hall stand and an elaborate old parlor organ.

These furniture kits are the ones you're most likely to find in retail stores. There are others, produced by

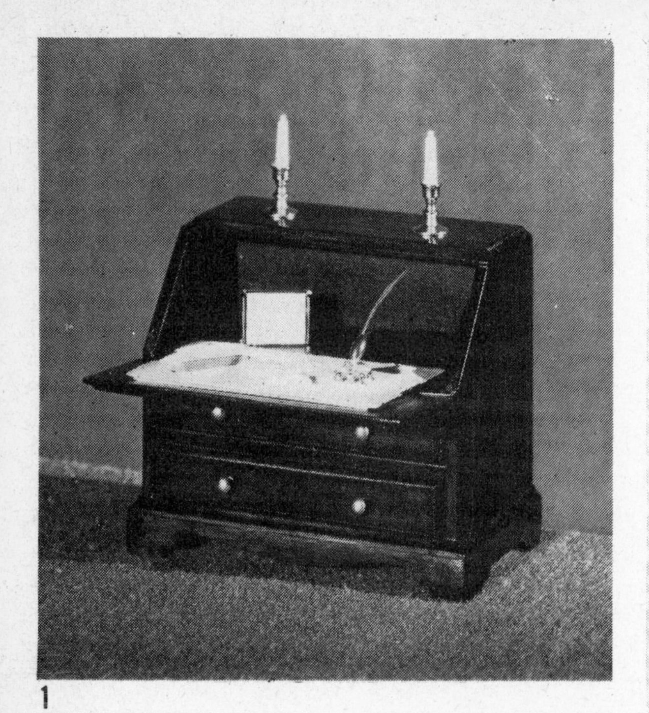

1

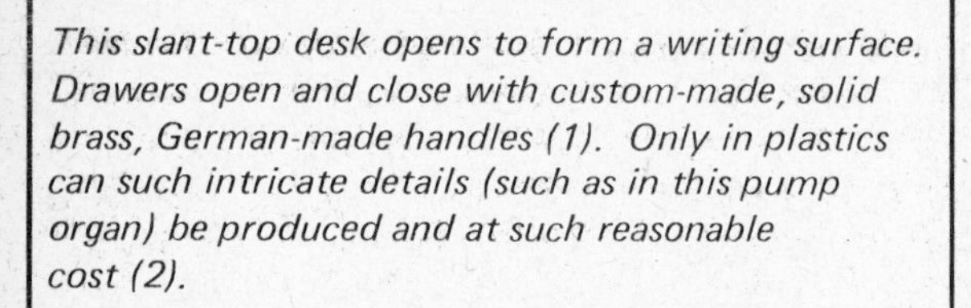

This slant-top desk opens to form a writing surface. Drawers open and close with custom-made, solid brass, German-made handles (1). Only in plastics can such intricate details (such as in this pump organ) be produced and at such reasonable cost (2).

2

individual craftsmen, that don't have a wide distribution, but they can often be purchased at miniature shows or through the mail. Some craftspeople have begun to package the parts for their specialties in kit form. Their products are often excellent.

But don't think that you need to follow the manufacturer's instructions exactly in assembling miniature furniture kits. Once you've become somewhat adept at putting pieces together, you might consider customizing them to make your own creation or to suit some special miniature setting. There's no need to use the material provided for upholstery, nor finish your furniture with the stain provided. Look at your kit-built furniture as though it were full-size, and you will begin to see the possibilities that kits offer.

For example, were you to purchase the Realife Miniatures dining room kit by Scientific Models, you would have all the components and materials needed to assemble a Colonial-style table with four chairs, a dry sink and a hutch. Instead of following the manufacturer's directions, you might make the set your own in several ways. If needlepoint is among your craft skills, make petit point chair seats. If folk painting is your passion, the dry sink would lend itself well to this type of embellishment. Instead of staining the piece with the color provided in the kit, use a lighter shade or paint the dry sink in a traditional color such as blue or ochre. Select a folk design that is relatively simple and reduce it to scale. With carbon paper, trace the design onto the doors of the dry sink and paint with acrylic paint. When dry, the entire piece can be "antiqued" with special solution from a craft shop.

Building from Scratch

Although there is a wide assortment of miniature furniture kits available, the time will undoubtedly arrive when you'll need a piece of furniture that has not been pre-cut and packaged. Or, from the beginning, you might prefer to work from your own ideas and designs instead of drawing upon someone else's. Either way, building miniature furniture from scratch isn't complicated.

Most miniature furniture consists of wood, fabric and metal, but miniatures—and miniaturists—cannot be

(Continued on page 25)

2

3

A fine collection of miniature silver and china is artfully displayed in this turn-of-the-century cabinet (1). This warm room is composed for an intimate afternoon of chamber music (2). Imagine this Victorian baby carriage parked on the stone patio of an elegant country mansion (3). A plain, three-story dollhouse is transformed and placed in period with the proper use of bricks, siding, shutters and doorway (4).

4

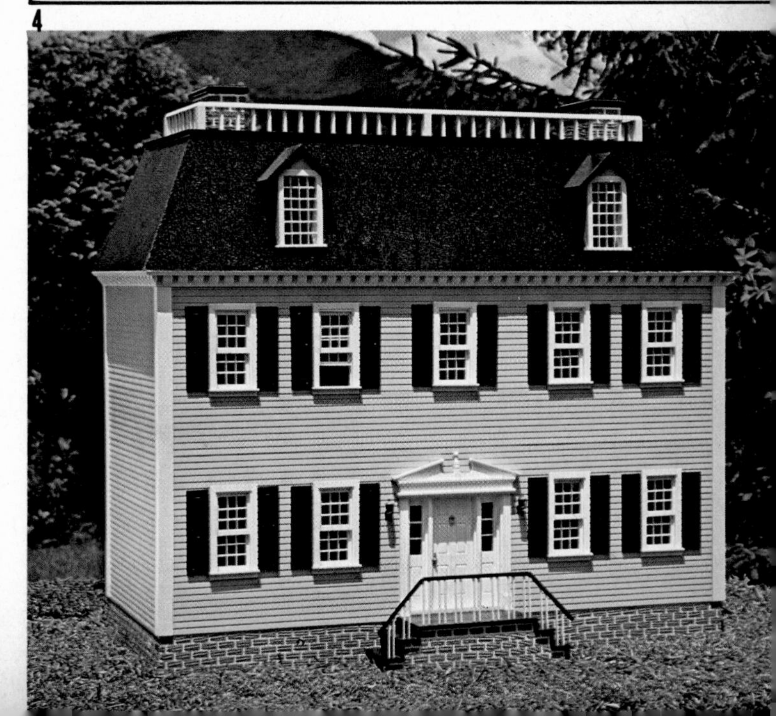

1

Although this modern acrylic room is stark and bare, it can come to life with the addition of books, plants, pillows and, perhaps, feathers in a floor vase (1). Dolls will be dolls and never little human beings, but in appropriate dress, they can fit well into a period room (2). Each item in this library adds to the total composition of the room. The pen and paper and carefully "tended" plants suggest imminent human activity (3). Even the decals and floor tiles of this '30s bathroom are to scale and carry the water theme. A bathrobe, slippers, a rug and a towel on the stool would give it the lived-in look (4).

2

3

4

1

2

This wedding shower shadow box might well become the most cherished momento of a happy event. Almost any interest -- from action sport to occupation -- lends itself to a miniature gift (1). Santa and Mrs. Claus are quite "at home" in this scene which shows off miniatures' variety. The whole package costs a tidy $1,176.50! (2). For needlework miniaturists, here are several items available in a single kit: a needlepoint rug, a Whig Rose quilt and pillow and a needlework picture for the wall (3). Nostalgia is the theme of this penny-candy shop and soda fountain. The candy-cane striped wallpaper and the red crank phone give one pause to recall a sweeter time (4).

3

4

1

2

Like a shop you might find on a narrow London street, this one displays miniature silver treasures behind a fifteen-light window. The pieces are further complemented by the brick and carved wood facade (1). Accented with tiny drawings, bolts of fabric with mini-prints and a dressmaker's dummy, this shadow box is a unique showroom for a special interest (2).

The World Of Miniatures

Be it ever so diminutive, there's no place like . . . Home is where the heart is . . . Many old sayings fit miniaturists' feelings about their hobby. The succeeding photographs illustrate the warmth of working with miniatures.

The wealth and elegance of pre-Revolution France is represented in the drawing room of the Colleen Moore Castle.

(Continued from page 16)

pinned down. Ingenious hobbyists have been known to incorporate all kinds of found objects into their furniture construction, all for the purpose of achieving that ultimate goal, the illusion of reality. At the same time, there are miniaturists whose purist approach demands that they employ only the authentic construction techniques used on full-size pieces. As a beginner, however, you should begin with simple materials and techniques, leaving the mortise and tenon joints for later.

Just as a beginning dressmaker would not likely attempt to design the pattern for her first garment, it's not advisable for you to devise your own furniture patterns until you've become fairly experienced at cutting and assembling miniatures. Fortunately, there are excellent books and magazines available which contain patterns and instructions for building a variety of miniature furniture pieces (see "Sources" for titles).

The best of these sources recommend beginning with a soft wood such as balsa or basswood. These woods can be purchased in sheets varying in thickness

These few and simple tools represent all you'll need to "raise" a house, fill it with furniture and hook up the lighting (1). These Early American pieces illustrate handmade or manufactured miniatures. Each may also be made from scratch using patterns from books and magazines (2). Plastics are popular because they are inexpensive and rich with detail (3).

1

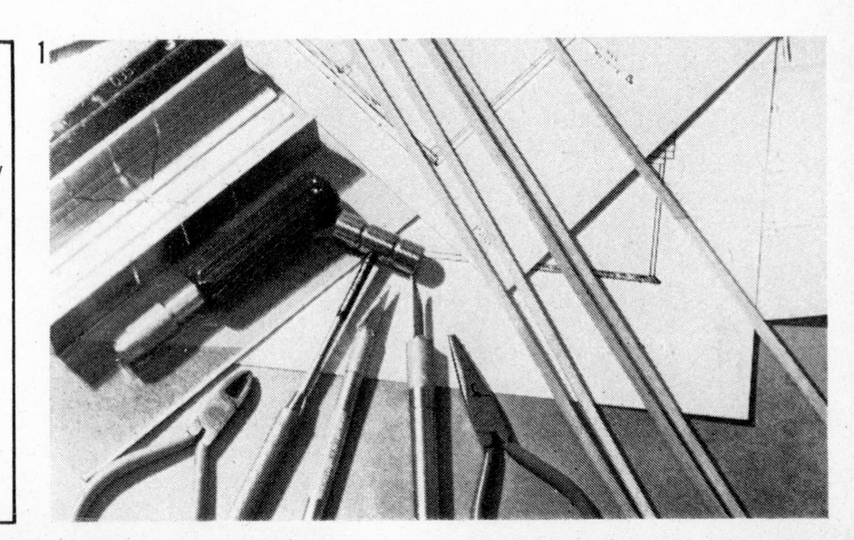

2

3

from one-thirty-second to one-quarter inch. (Generally one-eighth inch is recommended for miniature furniture.) You will also need an X-Acto knife with a No. 11 blade, a cutting board or surface, a metal-edged ruler, tracing and carbon paper, carpenter's glue, fine sandpaper, stain and varnish or paint. With these few materials, tools and patterns, you can easily construct your first miniature.

Select something simple with straight-lines for your initial project, trace the pattern from the book onto the tracing paper, then onto the wood using carbon paper. Place the wood on the cutting surface and cut out the pieces with the X-Acto knife, using your metal ruler as a guide on straight edges. Take care not to split the wood. When all the pieces have been cut out, gently sand the edges with sandpaper and try for a fit. This is the time to make adjustments or to cut new pieces if necessary. Stain them now, before they are glued together. (This construction sequence is a debatable issue among miniaturists; see "Techniques" for the alternate method.)

Using a toothpick, apply glue to one of the two sides that are to be jointed. Hold the two pieces together until the glue begins to set, then you can join the next piece.

Gluing should be done on a flat surface. Graph paper is helpful in lining up 90-degree angle sides.

1

2

3

A four-room shadow box is a good way to show off like-period pieces (1). The more-the-merrier-look of a Valentine's Day box demonstrates the ample opportunity to improvise with odds and ends (2). Turning out furniture like this polished table and benches can be a picnic! (3).

After the piece is fully assembled and the glue is thoroughly dry, it can be painted and/or varnished.

Simple as it is, this method of furniture building can be used to build almost every piece of furniture for your dollhouse. Experiment with making more ornately styled furniture. Consider working with balsa wood in solid blocks rather than in sheets and discover some of the things that can be done with carving. Try finishing the pieces with details of your own—dressmakers' eyes for drawer pulls, beads for finials, and carved dowels for table legs or bedposts. As you gain adeptness you will discover both possibilities and limitations.

Sooner or later, you may want to work with some "luxury" woods. For example, hardwoods make beautiful miniature furniture. They take stains as softwoods do not, and can be varnished and waxed to a finish comparable to any found on full-size furniture.

As soon as you begin to work with harder woods, you will need different tools. You might even consider investing in some of the power tools which skilled miniaturists find so useful. Power tools are not essential, and some of the best miniature furniture makers do not use them, but most miniaturists swear by multipurpose tools like the Dremel Moto-Shop workshop. Essentially a jigsaw, the Moto-Shop takes the drudgery

4

This clean and quality dry sink design has all the touches of fine, old-fashioned craftsmanship. Made of clear pine, it is available either unfinished or with a walnut stain (4). Improvisation shouldn't look like it. The framed flowers may be from an ad in a garden catalog, but are offered as though the picture were a print or an art "original" (5). This library bookcase and windowseat unit are actually two separate kits. The clear pine is hand-rubbed with a walnut finish (6).

5

6

out of many operations in miniature furniture making. For working in hardwoods, it's almost a must.

Among several other power tools which have been developed expressly for miniature work are lathes, sanders, saws and rotary tools; all vary widely in price. As your involvement in sanding, drilling, sawing, polishing and turning grows, you will likely see a need to add some of them to your workshop. In the meantime, small saws and other hand tools should suffice.

Scale Cabinetmaking

Perhaps it seems like nitpicking to differentiate between miniature furniture building and scale cabinetmaking. All miniature furniture is built to scale, true, but not all is representative of fine cabinetmaking. The only way to appreciate the difference is to get a look at that made by contemporary masters. Just as the fine touch shows on a full-size piece of furniture, so it is revealed in a miniature.

The finest miniature furniture is constructed exactly like its prototype. Where dovetailed joints are used on the original, they are used on the miniature. Inlays and carving are amazingly reproduced in one-twelfth size.

A china plate or pewter cup collection deserves display.

Drawers actually open, tables extend, beds have real roping. One scale cabinetmaker even constructed his secretary desk with a secret compartment that springs open at a touch.

Master craftspeople will go to unbelievable lengths. To furnish her reproduction of a seventeenth century house, one miniaturist discovered that the only way to duplicate the subtly colored textiles of the prototypes was to dye her fabrics with the same natural colors used by the Colonists. A maker of miniature musical instruments produces violins with real ebony pegs and sterling silver frog plugs in the bows. The bows are strung with human hair rather than horsehair, however, since the latter is too coarse to be in scale.

Such pinnacles of craftsmanship have been attained by individuals who began as hobbyists, often with little or no background in model making. One of the most accomplished scale cabinetmakers is a former plumber; another was a heavy machinery operator. Their perseverance and practice paid off in the tremendous development of their skill. They began where you begin. You, too, can develop your craft to such heights.

Accessories: Improvisation

It's in creating accessories for your miniature settings that your imagination will take off and all your powers of ingenuity will come into play. For many, the real fun of miniatures is in taking everyday objects from the "big" world and transforming them into functional and decorative dollhouse items. There is no end to the possibilities.

"Thinking small" is a matter of seeing things not as they are, but as they could be in one-twelfth scale. The seemingly insignificant takes on a whole new character and importance. Toothpaste caps become vases, bottle caps turn into pie tins or mixing bowls, buttons evolve to dishes or picture frames. One's old costume jewelry suddenly is a treasure trove of parts for lighting fixtures, drapery ornaments or dining utensils. Leftover bits of wood become wall sconces. Pill boxes, postage stamps, popsicle sticks — numberless, everyday, overlooked things are transformed by your new way of seeing the world. Pay attention to size, shape and texture, and soon everything that comes to hand will be seen for its potential in miniature.

The first step is to accumulate the "raw materials." It's not difficult; once you start collecting it can even become addictive. And, quickly, you will need a place to keep all your little "stuff." A plastic desk organizer placed inside a box, a partitioned fishing tackle box, a carton divided by smaller cartons—all are suitable. You might also find it worthwhile to purchase a chest of small plastic drawers especially made for storing hardware or hobby parts. Whatever you use, it should be compartmentalized to keep your odds and ends in order.

While you are organizing your bits and pieces you might also start a "mini thoughts and other trivia" file.

You'll be amazed at the ideas and information you can find in newspapers, magazines and catalogs. Buy an accordion file or a filing box to save your clippings.

Most odds and ends can be "scrounged," but here are some bought bits which could be handy for your improvisations: straight pins, thread, jewelry parts such as jump rings and bell caps, small gauge wire and miniature moldings in half-rounds and quarter-rounds. For tools and materials add tweezers, toothpicks, acrylic paints and paint brushes and several types of glue.

To bond different kinds of surfaces, you'll need assorted glues appropriate for a variety of jobs. Basic white craft glue, for example, is an excellent all-purpose glue. Some kit manufacturers provide white glue in their kits, but since white glue has been known to cause warping, most miniature furniture makers prefer a carpenter's glue. White glue is excellent, however, for adhering porous surfaces and paper and has the advantage of drying quickly.

A thicker type of white glue, sold under several trade names, comes in a jar and is useful for bonding fabrics and trimmings. It, too, will set up very quickly. A cement made especially for assembling plastic model kits is recommended. It can be purchased in any hobby shop or wherever plastic model kits are sold. An all-purpose clear glue is valuable for gluing dissimilar surfaces, such as metal and wood, to each other. For a very fast bond on hard-to-glue surfaces, you might want to add one of the cyanoacrylate glues to your supplies, but use them with caution; they can weld skin as well as metal.

With this collection of odds and ends, basic materials, tools and assorted glues, you have the means for improvisational miniaturing. Some suggestions are given below, but don't stop there. The items you make will be determined by the materials you collect and by your own imagination:

1. Cut pictures of magazines and books from advertisements to use as covers for miniature reading matter.
2. Use the soft leather from old gloves for book bindings, bedroom slippers, purses, upholstery and other items.
3. Save the balls from roll-on deodorants for chandelier lights or "coachlight" sconces.
4. Treasure those plastic gimcracks from gum ball machines and Cracker Jack snack boxes. (The party goods department of your local variety store is another good source.) Painted, they are effective as toys for a child's room or under the Christmas tree or even as decorative "art." "Bronzed" with a rub-on metallic paint and mounted on a stand, a plastic favor becomes a

Knots to you are the means to unique room decor for the needlecrafts miniaturists.

miniatures statuette to grace a mantel.

5. Look carefully at the packages of sugar in restaurants. Notice note cards, gift wrap, magazines and catalogs. Miniature art is everywhere.

6. Never throw away old compacts. You will want some mirrors for your dollhouse walls.

7. Use the embroidered corner of a hankie to make a lovely needlework wall hanging.

8. Glue one faceted bead from an old necklace to another to make a perfect boudoir lamp. Shape a cardboard shade and cover it with some gathered eyelet edging for a frilly, feminine accessory.

9. Top a simple brass lipstick tube with the cap from a bottle of roll-on deodorant for a larger, tailored lamp.

10. Place tiny dried flowers in a wooden bead for an attractive arrangement.

Some miniaturists feel that improvisation of this kind doesn't make fine, scale models, but others have produced excellent accessories by this inexpensive and imaginative method. Standards of scale should not be sacrificed in working with castoffs; "little" is simply not good enough. Even though a found part may seem to be perfect for a particular project, if it is out of scale, it isn't right. For examples of the heights which can be reached by improvisation, we recommend *The Book of Miniatures: Furniture and Accessories* by Helen Ruthberg. Written by an accomplished miniaturist, this book is a wellspring of ideas and instructions for creating all kinds of miniature accessories from unlikely items.

As we have shown, improvisation is just one approach to miniature making. Because it costs little and so challenges the imagination, it usually comprises a part of almost every miniaturist's hobby. Ideally, these miniatures should be so well-made that their humble origins cannot be detected. But for the sake of realism, don't use improvisation exclusively to accessorize a room or dollhouse. If overdone, it will become obvious and the intended effect will be lost.

Accessories: Crafts

Almost any kind of handwork that is used to produce full-size items can be done in miniature: metalcraft, ceramics, needlework, sculpture, macrame, painting, wood carving, glassblowing, quilling and many more. It can be an adventure to turn a pot or paint a picture one-twelfth the standard size. Some difficulties encountered in full-size crafts disappear in miniature, and some new ones arise. For instance, miniature macrame doesn't pose the problem of wrestling with yards of cord, but there's the new challenge in tying tiny knots.

It's not even necessary to be familiar with a craft in order to take it up in miniature. A miniature ceramicist once commented that, had she known much about the full-size craft, she would have regarded the problems of miniaturization insurmountable. On the other hand, knowledge of basic techniques is helpful.

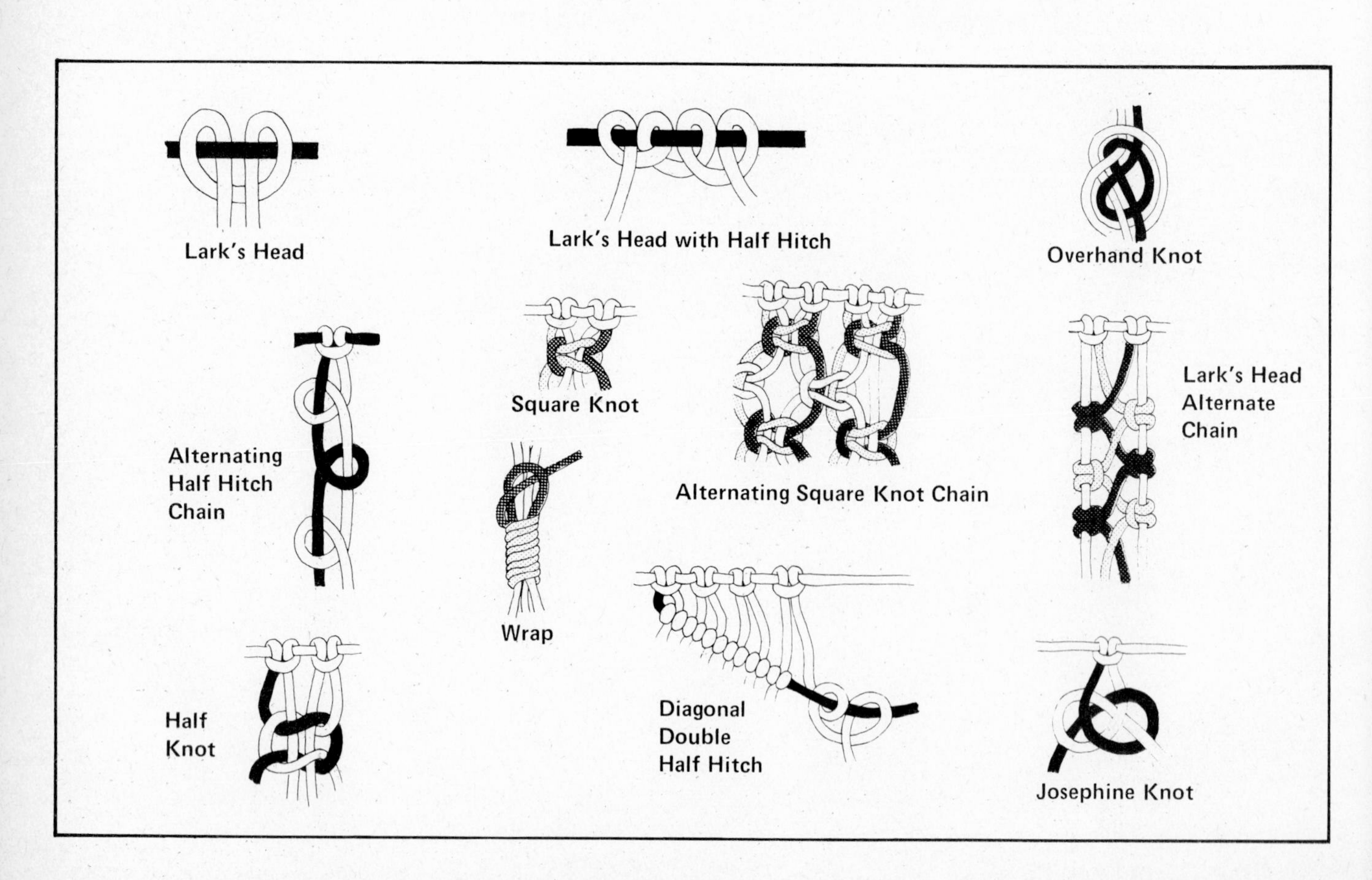

To adapt a craft to miniature work, first determine whether the materials are suitable for miniaturization. Clay, for instance, does not change its essential character from size to size. However, the glass, lead came and copper foil used for standard stained glass work are simply too large to produce miniature Tiffany lamps or stained glass windows to scale. The most realistic miniature "stained glass" work isn't even glass at all. Also, in some crafts, it may work best to substitute materials without changing technique. Reed isn't available in widths narrow enough to weave a one-twelfth size basket, but by substituting string or even thin strips of paper, a tiny one can be woven by full-scale basketweaving methods.

If you're not proficient in a craft, have dabbled in different ones without success or consider yourself "all thumbs" when it comes to handwork, don't be discouraged. Some of today's best miniature craftspeople never made anything before they began to work in miniatures.

The second step to creating craft accessories is to "bone up" on crafts. Read the general crafts magazines to acquaint yourself with the variety of crafts being practiced and to spark your imagination. Study the how-to articles and determine if the directions are applicable to miniature making and what changes or substitutions may have to be made. If a special craft strikes your fancy, read a book about it. Although few books have been written on specific crafts in miniature, hundreds have been published in recent years on every craft imaginable. You may also attend a workshop at a local craft studio in any one of the more popular crafts.

Lovely patterned miniature rugs are designed to fit rooms of various periods. Miniature carpets come in counted-thread cross-stitch, needlepoint, punch needle hooked and wall-to-wall varieties.

Needlecrafts and Fabrics

The majority of books on dollhouse miniatures discuss collecting and constructing miniatures, building and furnishing dollhouses and creating miniature room settings. The fact that miniature needlecraft is the only miniature craft to have had several books devoted to it is an indication of the importance of fabrics and needlecrafts in the completion of a miniature setting.

The most widely used needlecrafts include cross stitch, crewel and other embroidery techniques, punch needle, crochet, sewing and quilting. But petit point (very small needlepoint) is the queen of the miniature needle arts. Whereas a full-size house may contain one or two needlepoint accessories, a dollhouse will often abound with them—Persian carpets to firescreens, throw pillows to upholstered furniture. No other needlecraft achieves the realism and subtletly of color that petit point does. Worked on a No. 18 (18 stitches to the inch) or smaller single canvas, it usually employs three basic stitches (Basketweave, Continental and Gobelin). The challenge of the craft lies in their fineness.

Rugs. As in miniature furniture making, kits provide an excellent introduction to miniature needlecrafts. Several current lines of petit point kits provide materials, either prepainted canvas or a chart to follow and directions for making a miniature rug. The Tidewater Collection of Oriental Rug Kits from X-Acto's House of Miniatures offers an assortment of antique Oriental rugs, all in perfect proportion and of authentic design. Other firms feature petit point kits with designs for nursery, modern homes, etc. Complete directions for miniature needlepoint are included in *Needlework in Miniature* by Virginia Merrill and Jean Jessop. This book fully details every aspect of petit point for dollhouses and miniature rooms, and provides numerous charts for a variety of projects.

Other types of miniature needlework include counted-thread cross-stitch and crewel embroidery and punch needle. The punch needle method of hooking employs a miniature rug hook and produces charming, although somewhat thick, miniature rugs. Books showing Early American rooms are an excellent source of traditional patterns for this type of rug.

The braided rug is easily accomplished in miniature and will provide your period rooms with colorful floor coverings. Whereas full-size braided rugs are made from fabric cut in strips and braided together, miniature rug braiders substitute a lightweight knitting yarn. The braid is a simple three-strand braid executed with a light, even tension. The attractiveness of the rug depends upon the way the colors are combined. Most braided rugs are circles or ovals whose colors seem to flow from one shade to the next. Colors are joined by a small stitch, and when the braid is completed, the rug is sewn together from the center out. Care must be taken to keep the rug flat while sewing.

A braided rug is a fairly easy miniature craft project. With careful color planning, some bright and quaint floor coverings can be created.

Quilts. Probably the most beloved of all the folk arts, the patchwork quilt has also found its way into the dollhouse. If you are furnishing an early American bedroom or home, or even a later period farmhouse, these colorful bed coverings are an essential part of your interior decorating.

Quilts can be made by a number of methods to successfully suggest reality. Most quiltmakers prefer a simple nine-patch quilt made of one-inch squares sewn together. To piece a miniature quilt in the full-scale manner, however, can result in a rather stiff, thick covering. To avoid this, the most delicate fabrics must be selected for the squares and backing.

Silkscreening can successfully reproduce a more complicated quilt pattern. Silkscreened quilt tops, like piece quilt tops, are sewn to a fabric backing, given a thin cotton batten filling and stitched together by the usual quilting method. Placed on a bed, this special quilt can be most effective.

Silkscreened quilt tops in traditional American designs are available from Grandmother Stover's, the nation's oldest manufacturer of dollhouse miniatures. Add backing, edging and quilting stitches to these tops, and you have a very realistic "pieced" quilt. A number of individual craftspeople have packaged kits for making quilts, some pieced and some printed or silkscreened. Look for them at miniature shows.

Textiles. Properly planned, fabrics can go a long way toward lending realism to your miniature setting. But window treatments, bedding, upholstery and other "soft" aspects of interior decoration reflect the changes of fashion just as furniture does. So, when planning a period room, research the window coverings and other fabric accessories just as carefully as you do all the aspects of your developing room.

An incorrect fabric destroys the illusion of realism in miniatures almost as much as out-of-scale accessories...the tiny quilt that refuses to conform to the shape of the bed, draperies that puff out awkwardly from windows. The cause is often the use of fabric that is either too heavy or too resistant to the shaping and draping required of it. As a general rule, very fine fabric woven of natural fiber is most suitable for a dollhouse. Check the necktie rack for a marvelous source of soft, malleable silk, the handkerchief counter of your nearest department store for fine, lightweight cotton in many colors and patterns. Look closely at the trimmings in a yard goods store. A fine one- or two-inch wide lace makes an ideal dresser scarf or could be made into curtains or table cloths. Always look for the thinnest and most flexible materials. If you have some concern about whether or not a fabric is too heavy, it probably is.

But making your own miniatures may not appeal to you. And perhaps your visit to a miniatures shop or show turns up just the right pieces to finish a room. With your first purchase, you become a collector, and your "small" world expands.

1

2

Miniature cloth must be light so it will lay softly along furniture lines (1). Patterns of mini-textiles must also be to-scale, and the design must be appropriate to the period represented (2).

Collecting Miniatures

This miniatures shop displays affordable elegance.

BEFORE THERE WAS a hobby called "miniatures," there was one called "miniatures collecting" made up of a little-known group of enthusiasts. Once regarded by their friends as eccentrics, they were supplied with items for their collections by an even smaller group of miniatures craftspeople who worked without acclaim and without much recompense for their efforts.

All that has changed. Sometime around the beginning of the 1970s, the collecting of miniatures suddenly caught on, and it has been growing ever since. (For our purposes, "collecting" is defined as buying, as opposed to making.) Almost overnight it has become the subject of countless books, articles and shows that attract thousands of visitors. Appealing to large numbers of people on different intellectual and emotional levels, the collecting of miniatures clearly has the power to captivate people in a way that the collecting of thimbles, teacups, stamps or coins cannot.

Miniatures collecting is not regarded as an activity separate from and unrelated to that larger hobby called "miniatures." Collecting and crafting miniatures go hand in hand. You may collect more than you create or vice versa, but you'll probably do both.

There are several ways to approach miniatures collecting. You can collect pieces only to fulfill the purpose of finishing a planned room or dollhouse; you can collect antique miniatures for themselves or as possible investments; or you can concentrate on contemporary miniatures of quality, investing in their probable appreciation. Finally, you may decide to collect according to a subject, a medium or a historical period. Include at least one of these ways in your master plan.

A miniature collection begins with the first purchase, be it a piece of furniture or an accessory. Many of these pieces will be handcrafted, others will be manufactured. You will undoubtedly find a place for both in your collection.

Judging Quality

Good quality is important to any collection. It, too, promotes realism. You should judge each prospective purchase in terms of scale, materials, detail and design. These standards apply to all miniatures, manufactured and handcrafted.

Judging the accuracy of the scale of a miniature

1

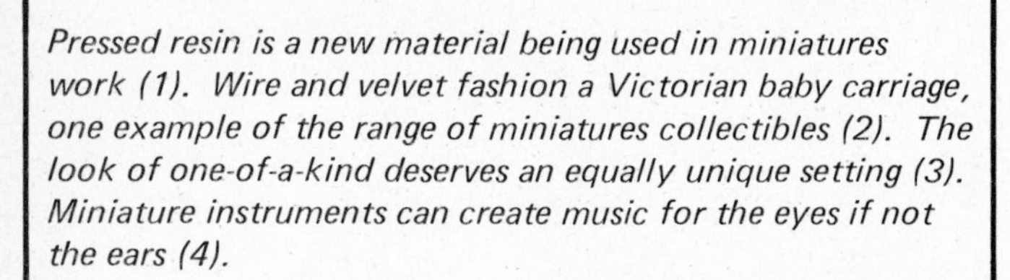

Pressed resin is a new material being used in miniatures work (1). Wire and velvet fashion a Victorian baby carriage, one example of the range of miniatures collectibles (2). The look of one-of-a-kind deserves an equally unique setting (3). Miniature instruments can create music for the eyes if not the ears (4).

2

piece involves more than simply determining whether the general dimensions are properly scaled. Check details such as chair legs and splats, fabric coverings and trimmings and wood grain. Some very fine woods have grains that are simply too large for miniatures. In time, you'll be able to spot discrepancies in scale without having to resort to a ruler.

Design and detail are a bit more difficult to judge. As a beginning collector, each piece in miniature may seem to be the ultimate in precision. You may become enchanted with one fine replica only to discover another representation of the same type of miniature in which the detail far surpasses the first. As you are exposed to more and better work, your standards will rise. For this reason, you should take every opportunity to view all kinds and qualities of miniatures. This will refine your tastes and tune your perception of quality.

Your evaluation of miniatures design will be greatly influenced by your personal tastes and objectives. In the beginning, if you focus your collecting upon a particular period, style or theme you will learn to judge design within those limitations and will create parameters for your buying. For example, if you decide to collect only Victorian furniture and accessories, you should study as much as you can about the interiors and furniture styles of that period. You will then be able to determine whether a piece of miniature furniture is accurately representative and what kind of room it is likely to be found in. It will also add to your enjoyment of the piece. Accuracy still allows for that elusive quality called personal taste. Judging design may just come down to whether or not a certain piece appeals to you. If it does, and you can afford it, buy it.

Determining the quality of the materials used in miniatures is another subjective element in selection. To a large extent, your judgment will depend upon how much of a purist you are. The purists maintain that authenticity is absolutely essential. They will never be satisfied with anything but authentic materials, and plastic miniatures are an anathema. However, some outstanding craftspeople hold that illusion and effect are the miniaturist's goal and that anything which achieves that goal is acceptable. One company named Chrysnbon is built upon that premise. Their miniatures, exquisite in detail and at reasonable prices, are made almost entirely from plastic.

As a new collector, no doubt with budget limitations, you must decide whether to buy a quantity of average products or to limit your collecting to a smaller number of first-rate miniatures. If you regard miniature collecting primarily as an investment, it's no contest. Although the main thrust of the hobby isn't in this direction, it's becoming increasingly evident that miniatures are as viable an investment as other types of art. Know-

3

4

knowledge of craftspeople and appreciation of the works is essential if you are to pursue this course. You should know names like Buttfield, Kupjack, McKnight, Farnsworth, Van Horn and Prescott, who are among the best in the field. You'll also need the financial resources with which to purchase their products; they're not cheap. A secretary desk made by Don Buttfield, for instance, will command close to $2,000. The pleasure of owning such a piece is enhanced by its obvious present value and the promise of its worth in the future.

Manufactured Miniatures

The manufacture of miniatures began in 1940. It was then that John Stover formed a company, called Grandmother Stover's, that manufactured accessories for children's dollhouses. The business was the outgrowth of Stover's own efforts to supply his three young daughters with items for their dollhouses. His fertile imagination and the hands of home craftspeople are still the source for such items as tiny balls of yarn for miniature knitting baskets, framed pictures, braided rugs and other homey touches for dollhouse kitchens and other rooms. Grandmother Stover's miniatures are moderately priced; most items sell for under $2. They are not fine miniatures, but they add those finishing touches so important to authenticity.

Most miniatures manufacturers design their products in this country but have them manufactured abroad, usually in either Taiwan or South America. One exception to this is Perfection Products Company, manufacturers of the Americana in Miniature line of furniture. Available in both kits and finished form, the pieces are produced from hard maple in a factory in North Carolina. (Grandmother Stover's pieces are manufactured in Ohio.) A newcomer to the miniatures field, the prestigious Goebel Company (creators of the Hummel figurines), has recently introduced a line of pressed resin furniture which is finely detailed and also manufactured entirely in the United States. A list of other manufacturers can be found in the "Sources" section at the end of this book.

Handcrafted Miniatures

Although the miniatures hobby has grown at an astonishing rate recently, in many respects it remains a cottage industry. The vast majority of suppliers of both materials and completed items are individual craftspeople or "Mom and Pop" operations. Indeed, the individual craftsperson is the backbone of the hobby.

Miniature work is done in every conceivable medium to keep collectors supplied with everything from the dollhouses themselves down to the salt and pepper shakers for the dining room table. Each craftsperson has a specialty and each specialty has its own "stars"—those whose work is considered the best in its medium and usually commands the highest prices.

Handmade products are marketed in various ways. Some miniatures artists wholesale their products to a select group of dealers who, in turn, sell them only at miniatures shows. Others prefer to enter shows themselves, exhibiting their own work and personally taking orders. There are loners whose customers only know them by mail and others who combine show sales with direct mail orders. And miniature shops are sales rooms for some who work on commission.

Although local miniatures shows displaying the works of local people contain some fine examples of miniature making, to see and have access to the works of the stars among craftspeople, you must attend one of the prestigious shows of the field. Shows sponsored by the National Association of Miniatures Enthusiasts (N.A.M.E.), the Miniatures Makers' Society and the Midwest Miniatures Trade Association provide you with an opportunity to see the work of the top people in the hobby and to establish good standards and guidelines for purchasing the works of lesser known artists. Because there are new craftspeople continually joining the miniatures ranks, you may be one of the lucky ones to buy the work of an excellent craftsperson before he or she is "discovered."

For the professional craftsperson, the problem presented by the infringement of correspondence and business administration upon working time is a serious one. As the demand for the work increases, the craftsperson also faces difficulties in fulfilling orders. And the backlog situation worsens when customers' inquiries regarding their orders must be answered. As a collector, you should be aware that this situation exists especially among those doing custom work. Most of the more experienced professionals will advise you about delays for delivery. If you are not so advised, ask the craftsperson how long your order will take to be filled. A reply to your initial inquiry will undoubtedly be expedited if you enclose a self-addressed stamped envelope or a post card with appropriate responses to be checked by the artist and returned to you.

But be prepared to wait. If their work is top quality and the world of miniatures has beaten a path to their door, you must take your turn.

1

2

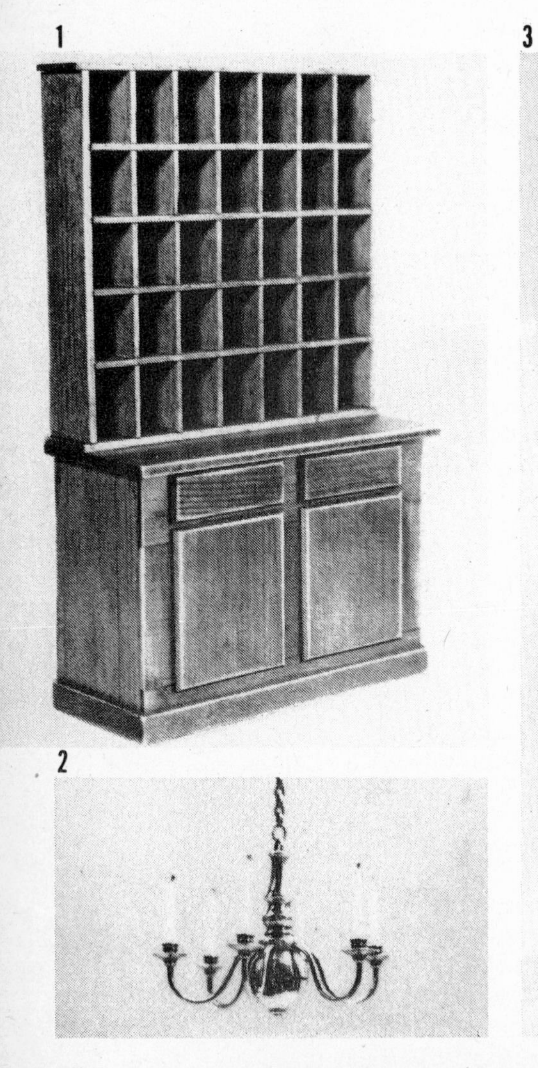

3

Shops and Mail-Order Houses

Not long ago, miniatures shops were few and far between, and mail-order houses specializing in miniatures were almost nonexistent. Today, *Miniature Dealer,* the business trade magazine, estimates that there are 5,000 retail stores handling miniatures. Miniatures may comprise their total inventory or may be relegated to a corner of the department including macrame, crafts supplies and even model railroad equipment. In a craft-related miniatures store, you will find handmade and manufactured miniatures, furniture kits, building components, wallpaper, paint and a variety of tools important to the miniature work. The store owners may also offer workshops in miniature making or may even be a means to get in touch with individual local craftspeople who give classes.

No two shops are alike. Because of miniatures' small size, even a tiny shop can contain a huge selection, and frequently a single shop will be the sole retail outlet for a particular craftsperson. A visit to any one of the thousands in the country can prove rewarding.

Since some miniatures manufacturers have begun exhibiting at shows for the gift, novelty and toy trades, many other kinds of shops also carry miniatures. You'll be surprised at some of the places where they turn up for sale. If you should encounter miniatures in an unlikely shop, check the scale of the items carefully; they may be offered as novelties rather than as scale reproductions.

An even greater selection of merchandise can often be found between the pages of a mail-order catalog. It is the foundation upon which the hobby was built and continues to grow. With a well-rounded library at your fingertips, you have access to the work of most of the professional craftspeople and to all the kits, materials and tools you'll need for your miniature crafting.

Almost everyone in the miniatures business has a catalog. Most manufacturers have a consumer book even though they don't always sell directly to the public, and many retail stores run a mail-order business in conjunction with their shop. Most professional craftspeople at least have a price list of their own work, and some of them conduct a direct mail business for their own and others' work. Each catalog is different, and each is fascinating in its own way.

A catalog's price is not always a reliable guide to its comprehensiveness or quality, however. Many mail-

4

5

This rural "post office" suggests miniatures' availability by mail (1). Light from this sterling silver chandelier would warm a tiny vestibule (2). There are miniaturists who are music lovers, too (3). Baked goods are tantalizingly displayed in a crafted case (4). A typical miniatures shop offers dollhouses and accessories (5).

order companies are nothing more than basement operations with all the purchasing, order fulfillment and catalog publishing done by one or two individuals. Such small businesses cannot afford to absorb any of the catalog printing or mailing costs, so must charge their customers top dollar for the catalogs even though the books may be smaller and less professionally produced than those offered by larger companies for less money. In spite of the fact that these seemingly overpriced catalogs are frequently poorly illustrated and sometimes even handwritten, they often contain unusual items that are available nowhere else.

First, order one of the large retail catalogs from a company handling a wide range of supplies for the miniatures hobby: dollhouses and/or dollhouse kits, furniture kits, dollhouse components, completed furniture, electrification supplies, tools, lighting fixtures, and accessories. It may not offer everything you'll need but will prove an excellent source for most of the products from the major manufacturers in the field. Later, you can search out some of the more specialized catalogs, those of individual craftspeople or small mail-order houses handling exclusive lines.

Dollhouse Dolls

Just as there is a sharp division between the purists and the illusionists, there are also two very definite opinions regarding dolls in miniature settings. It may seem ludicrous to suggest that dolls have no place in a dollhouse, but miniaturists are quick to point out that the word "dollhouse" is an old one which has not yet been supplanted by the more mature-sounding "miniature home" or "model house."

Since the ultimate goal of the miniaturist is to reproduce reality with a precision that deceives the eye, the illusion could never be achieved were a doll placed in the scene; the human figure defies miniaturization. No matter how carefully crafted, a doll is a doll, and not a miniature human being.

If you wish to merely suggest human habitation, there are hundreds of ways in which this can be achieved. A table set for dinner, a fire flickering in the fireplace, gloves on a table, a child's toy on the floor, all these speak of a room's resident, close by and about to enter. Such touches lend warmth and charm and prevent a room or dollhouse from being merely a sterile model.

Even though the perfect dollhouse doll has never been nor probably ever will be created, you still may wish to populate your settings. A miniature figure can serve to illustrate the customs, lifestyle and dress of a historical period or add a special touch to a nostalgic scene. "Grandmother's Kitchen" and "Smith's General Store" might come even more to life if the appropriate character dolls are included in the settings.

Of course, realism is the most desirable quality to look for in a dollhouse doll. There are imported German dolls on the market which have flexible bodies and lifelike features. Available fully clothed, they can also be re-dressed in whatever period or fashion you choose. The dolls are carried by many miniatures shops or mail order firms. Recently introduced to the market is a line of Victorian dolls in various poses. Although their positions cannot be changed, they look very natural in a 19th century setting. Several professional craftspeople produce perfectly scaled and detailed dolls especially for dollhouses. Like all fine handcrafted miniatures, these dolls are rather expensive, but the best of them are lovely and as realistic as it is possible for a doll to be.

Regardless of whether or not you choose to populate your miniature room or dollhouse with dolls, there is really only one answer to the question, "Who will live there?" As it draws near completion, a miniature setting or dollhouse reflects a special life all its own. It is the expression of your interests, your talents, your memories and your dreams. Obviously, there is really only one person who can live in that Lilliputian world that you created: You.

1

2

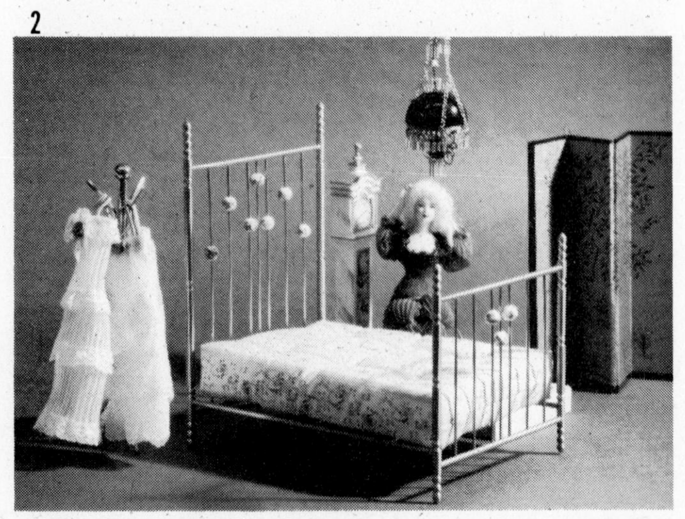

Dolls can stand alone or enhance a certain setting (1). Even a "real doll" is still not a tiny person (2).

Housing Your Hobby

A modern dollhouse provides the latitude for multi-period decorating.

WITHOUT A SETTING, miniatures lack completeness and meaning. It is when they are viewed in relation to one another, in a unified milieu, that the frequently used term, "the world of miniatures," is fully understood.

Creating a miniature setting is not unlike painting a picture. It requires planning and some feeling for composition and color. But because it is three-dimensional, the completed setting has a realism that most paintings do not possess. It is as though a moment in time has been captured and reduced in size. There is a projection of both reality and unreality, and therein lies the fascination.

The Master Plan

Whatever the elusive quality is that sets some miniature settings above others, that something extra that might be called "charm" or "beauty," it is the result of careful planning. It is planning that gives a room harmony, unity and authenticity. Although careful planning may slow down your progress in some respects, in other ways it will simplify the work and make it more successful in the end. Think in terms of theme (period or mood), composition and color scheme. What is it you wish to accomplish in each of these areas?

Theme. Having selected your theme, write down the period and function of the room you are planning. Next, write down the pieces of furniture that you consider most essential for the room. Make a second list of the accessories and less important pieces of furniture that you would like to include. Add a notation next to each item indicating whether you already possess it or if you intend to buy or make it yourself.

Now is the time to begin any research you may deem necessary in order to assure the authenticity of your room. Look in your local library for books on the furniture and customs of the period. As you read you may turn up some little known fact that can be incorporated into your room to make it even more interesting and authentic.

Composition. Composition plans will relate how and where your selected furnishings and accessories will go in a room. Thumbnail sketches help. Draw the floor dimensions to scale to make sure that the sketch will correspond to the planned room. For instance, if your room is to be twelve by eighteen inches, your sketch could be four by six inches. (Divide both dimensions by three.) Allow for doors and windows and any other set features in the room. On the floor plan, sketch in where you intend to place the major and essential pieces of furniture. Divide these dimensions by three also. A cabinet measuring one and a half inches deep by three inches wide would occupy a space one-half by one inch in your sketch.

This bird's eye view of your furnished miniature room will show how everything is going to fit and will let you make changes in room size or furniture pieces before you even begin. If your eye for perspective is keen you can also make sketches of the room from straight on and from an angle. This will give you a fairly clear idea of what your completed room will look like.

Color scheme. It is often the effective use of color that gives a room the unity that sets it apart from others of its kind. In fact, it's possible to achieve more with color in miniature than in full-size. One reason is that it's often easier to carry it out. And, because the eye can take it all in at once, the impact of the color scheme, like the palette of a painting, is stronger. Through the use of color you can accentuate one part of the setting, creating a center of interest. For example, if a room is decorated in subtle brown and gold tones and a bright orange couch is introduced, the couch will dominate and draw the eye to its area first.

Naturally, some periods will permit more latitude in the matter of color than will others. The early Americans didn't have color schemes as we do in our homes today. Still, it is possible to plan a color scheme even within the confines of that period. You may, for example, keep all the dishes, crockery, quilts, coverlets, floor coverings and table cloths in tones of blue.

The selection of a dominant color for a room of any period will go a long way to giving it a unified look. Next, consider colors complementary to the dominant hue and whether those colors will be bright, light or subdued. Will the room look best in warm colors (red, yellow, orange), or should it be decorated in cool tones (blue, green, lavender)? Play with some colored pencils or crayons. Make a large square of one color and draw smaller swatches of other colors next to it.

When you find an appealing color combination, consider its application to your room. List all the items from your theme list which will be in that color. Don't forget floor coverings, draperies, wallpaper and furniture upholstery; these are areas where color selection is of primary importance.

(Continued on page 49)

1

2

Theme is an important factor in miniatures planning (1). Elegant wallpaper and a period fireplace form a backdrop for an impending Sunday afternoon soiree (2). A glass bell protects a party set from dulling dust (3).

3

1

4

1

A prime place for peeping miniaturists is The Colleen Moore Castle in Chicago (1). Chippendale is a big name in any size. This hardwood frame couch is covered with velvet upholstery (2). This stair-step style table holds an eclectic array of items in a miniature collection (3).

2

3

Reproducing the very colors and designs of antique orientals and other fine carpeting, these miniature rugs would warm any room (1). This drop leaf table and pair of ladder-back chairs are against the wall now but, at Thanksgiving, can be set up with a full feast complete with turkey, pies and centerpiece (2). Seventeenth century Italian furniture, made in Columbia, So. America, fill this three-story dollhouse (3).

2

3

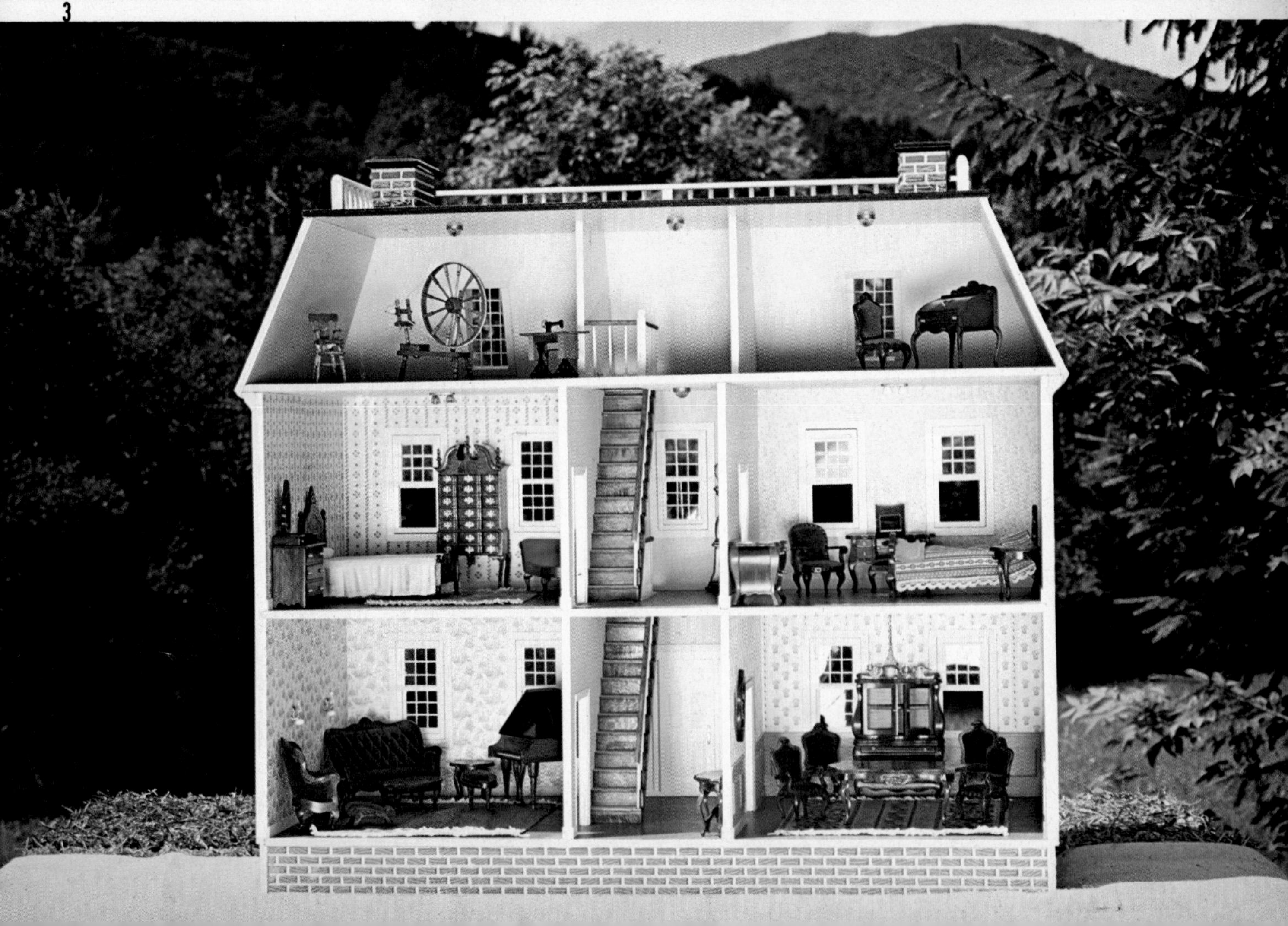

1

2

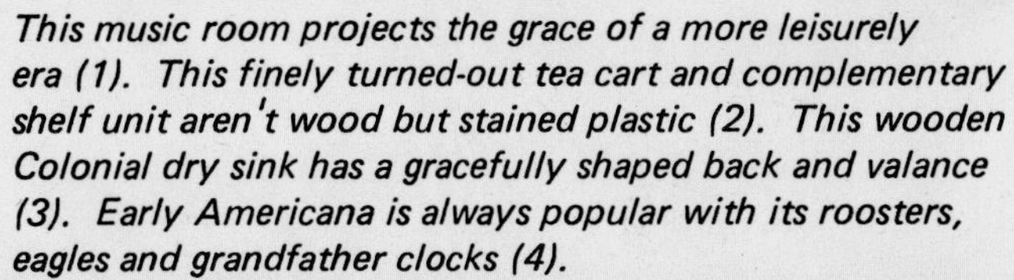

This music room projects the grace of a more leisurely era (1). This finely turned-out tea cart and complementary shelf unit aren't wood but stained plastic (2). This wooden Colonial dry sink has a gracefully shaped back and valance (3). Early Americana is always popular with its roosters, eagles and grandfather clocks (4).

3

2

3

The Colleen Moore Castle chapel suggests a grandeur far beyond its size. Make-believe monarchs might have been crowned here (1). This hardwood grandfather clock, made from a kit, is a copy and can be bought with a working electronic watch movement which will keep accurate time for a year (2). Although this small setting is all made of plastic, it has the look of hardrock maple, which fits the Early American style (3).

OF THE DECLARATION OF INDEPENDENCE
UNITED STATES OF

Small Is Beautiful

To be tiny isn't enough. A true miniature is a scale model of a full-size house, room or piece of furniture. The resulting illusion makes you feel that if you found a bottle marked "drink me," you'd find yourself right at home

The color in this country kitchen reflects the warmth of the original. Note the subtle red,white and blue touches.

(Continued from page 40)

Follow-Through. A plan is only as good as its execution. Without applying it to the actual development of a room or dollhouse, it remains an unrealized dream.

Careful planning of your miniature room or dollhouse by means of lists and sketches will greatly facilitate your miniature collecting and crafting. Lilliput, like the real world, is easier to find your way around in when you know where you're going. If you have followed the suggestions given here, you will have a list including every item needed in each setting, along with specifications for color and style. Next time you attend a miniatures show or visit a shop, take the list with you. You'll avoid buying something that you don't really have a place for. On the other hand, always be open to surprises—the perfect mininature that is exactly right even though you hadn't thought to put it on your list. Follow your plan but be flexible. Some of the most effective rooms includes happy "accidents."

Whether you are a master miniature cabinetmaker, an odds and ends improvisor or strictly a collector, the arrangement of your miniatures in a meaningful display is your goal. As you begin to acquire pieces, you will probably form some ideas for exhibiting them. There are three conventional types of display from which to choose: the shadow box, the miniature room and the dollhouse. Eventually your involvement may include all three, but the question now is where to begin.

Shadow Boxes

A shadow box is a shallow, enclosed case, usually set in a frame and faced with glass. Its depth of two or three inches can accommodate some pieces of miniature furniture—chairs, occasional tables, a chest of drawers and so forth—but is insufficient for large pieces like canopy beds and dining tables.

At first glance, the shadow box may seem to be too limited a vehicle for even the beginning miniaturist. At

4

5

6

A bare-bones doctor's office calls for cheerful wallpaper to set it off (4). Weathered shingles and window boxes, and a Cape Cod dollhouse becomes a home (5). America's favorite city provides a favorite house style -- Little Frisco (6).

1

best, it represents only a portion of a room. Nevertheless, you will discover that the shadow box has some distinct advantages over larger display cases. It is the perfect means by which to create a three-dimensional illustration. It lends itself especially well to the portrayal of a theme or to the vignette, and hung on a wall, it takes up no more room than an ordinary picture.

A shadow box is the least complex of all miniature display cases. It is easily constructed from wood or can be improvised from a cheese box, an old clock case or a cigar box. There are also several firms which manufacture shadow boxes especially for crafts and miniatures.

Because a shadow box is shallow, the items within it can be viewed with ease and under no special lighting. A small miniature collection or a personalized gift that expresses the interests and special memories of its recipient are best housed in shadow boxes. A scene might incorporate a model ship for a sailing enthusiast, a flower arrangement for a gardener, a cat or dog reminiscent of a family pet, a pennant from a university or college, sports equipment, tools, books, photographs, and so forth. Shadow boxes also enable you to isolate and focus on details which might be overlooked in a larger, more complex miniature setting. A fine piece of miniature furniture of which you are proud might best be exhibited in a shadow box where it can be the center of interest.

Finally, in creating a shadow box scene, you will gain practice in many of the techniques used in decorating a dollhouse or full miniature room. The inside walls must be painted or papered and a covering placed over the floor. Details must be coordinated and the full box planned for best effect.

A shadow box is not the only way to become involved with miniatures, but it may be the simplest way with a minimum investment. And by the time you've completed your first shadow box, you'll know

2

3

Quaint clutter is one of the charms of miniature rooms. You can "say it all" in your small space (1). Shadow boxes are just right for snatches of life like this wedding party box complete with champagne and wrapped presents (2). A four-story Georgian townhouse, with its wrought iron porch railings, is prime for fitting out with antique miniatures (3).

whether or not you want to go on to bigger and better things.

Miniature Rooms

Like many miniaturists, you may find the miniature room a favorite and stay with it exclusively. Miniature rooms offer both variety and convenience. Each is a separate entity and, once completed, can be displayed on a shelf by itself or with other rooms. Unlike the rooms of a dollhouse, a collection of miniature rooms need not relate to one another in historical period or function. The miniature room gives you a freedom of expression. You can recreate a scene from the past with every detail historically accurate. You can assemble the living room of your dreams and recapture the kitchen of your childhood.

Whatever your plan, you must first begin with a box. If woodworking is not among your craft skills, there is a wide selection of boxes for miniatures available by mail or from miniatures shops. They range from a very simple, three-sided box to more elaborate ones with glass or one-eighth inch acrylic sheet fronts and frames around the viewing area. The boxes come in several different sizes; generally, a miniature room is about 12 inches deep and 12 to 20 inches wide. But, the dimensions you select will be determined by the room you've planned, how much it will contain, etc. If you opt to make the box yourself, there are books available which give complete directions for its construction (see "Sources" at the end of this book).

Once you have your basic box, you're ready to begin "miniaturing" in earnest. By now, you have decided upon the theme of your room and have some idea of the items to be placed in it. It isn't necessary to have any furniture or accessories yet, and even if you do have some, they cannot be put into the room until the interior (paint, wallpaper, flooring, moldings, windows

1

2

A stairway style should match the rest of a dollhouse's architecture (1). White stucco and wood laths define this English Tudor dollhouse (2). Landscaping adds to dollhouse authenticity (3).

and doors) is complete. Also, at this point you must decide whether you wish the room to be lighted and by which method.

The necessity for lighting will vary, depending upon the dimensions of the box. Because a miniature room possesses depth, lighting of some kind aids in visibility and generally makes the room more attractive and realistic. If you place glass over the top and the front of the box, you will increase the viewing area and eliminate the need for artificial light. But if an opaque ceiling is used you will probably require some form of lighting in your room.

The box can be lighted by tiny fluorescent lights placed under the top of the frame or by electrification of the lighting fixtures which make up part of the setting. There are several firms which deal in nothing but lighting and electrification components for miniatures. These have been greatly simplified for the person inexperienced in electricity. Electrification of your miniature room, although not essential, definitely enhances it.

Your planning and careful progress will pay off as you watch your idea begin to take form. As you add each detail you will become more involved in the pleasure of your new hobby.

Dollhouses

For some, only a dollhouse will do. If you're one of those to whom a dollhouse is an object of longing, a secret desire, or the pot of gold at the end of the rainbow, then perhaps you should begin here. However, remember: a dollhouse is a commitment. Not only does it represent a sizable financial investment, but there is also a commitment to a particular period and to a given number of rooms which must be completed. But if you are the persevering type, then for you a dollhouse may be the ideal entry into the miniatures hobby.

The initial step is to acquire the basic house. There are two major decisions to be made at this point. The first is to determine which period you wish the house to represent. (If you do not have strong feelings about this, it is probably best not to begin with a dollhouse.) A dollhouse is an integral whole. Its rooms must all relate to one another, and they should all be of the same

3

period. To furnish a dollhouse with a Victorian parlor and an Early American kitchen, for instance, simply doesn't work. The only way one can get around this restriction is by working with a modern-day house and furnishing the rooms in various periods just as people do their full-size homes. In this case, you would be obliged to equip your dollhouse with a modern kitchen and bath for authenticity.

The second decision to be made in acquiring a dollhouse is whether to buy or to build the house. Side issues are: how much of the work do you wish to do yourself, and how much money are you able and willing to spend.

Building a house. If you decide to build, you may select a dollhouse from one of the many kits currently on the market. Three popular architectural styles dominate dollhouse kits: Colonial, Victorian and "farmhouse." Some are quite elaborate, and most have been designed by knowledgeable people. Each comes complete with walls, doors, windows, stairways, roof and complete instructions for assembly. Prices range from $50 to $400.

To select a kit of good quality, look at the component parts carefully. Are the walls thick and sturdy? Do the windows work? Do the pieces fit together squarely? Are the moldings, doors, hinges and flooring materials exactly what you want? Of course, a kit is only a shell and you will make alterations as your skills increase, but you will be happiest if you start out with the best basic house you can afford in the period, style and size of your wishes.

There's another way to build your own dollhouse . . . without using a kit and without becoming a union carpenter. A number of companies and individuals are now producing dollhouse plans—instruction sheets and patterns for construction—in a wide choice of styles. Although it will take longer to build a dollhouse this way, and you will have to track down and buy all the materials yourself, the completed house will be more detailed and probably less expensive than one built from a kit.

With experience in carpentry and some definite ideas about what you want, you've another dollhouse building option open to you—you can design and construct the whole house yourself. Such a project should not be undertaken lightly, however. Before you begin, study all that it takes to be your own architect, builder, roofer, electrician, painter, etc. Read some of the current books written on the subject and study the plans included or buy a separate set of plans to get an idea of all that is involved in dollhouse construction. This approach to dollhouse building is not recommended for the average beginner, but it is well within the capabilities of those with cabinetmaking experience or other construction or modeling skills.

Buying a House. The miniatures hobby has grown to such proportions that there are several house builders working full-time turning out custom-made dollhouses and a number of manufacturers producing ready-made, fully assembled ones. The choice is a wide one, beginning with a small, simple "shell" priced at under $100 up to fully detailed and decorated "mini mansions" constructed by master builders and costing thousands of dollars.

Before the Civil War, the people of the Old South lived lives of style and grace. The Southern Plantation dollhouse, above, is a replica of a mansion from that era. Made of ponderosa pine, the six-room dollhouse calls for Williamsburg furniture inside and wicker swings and hanging plants against traditional white painted siding. A gazebo would be a grand touch.

Even on a small scale, building materials are going up in price; everything costs more than anticipated. And as a dollhouse builder you must also pay yourself for your time. Estimate the hours required to build a dollhouse, multiply that by a reasonable hourly wage, add the cost of materials, and you will see how easy it is to spend $200 on a ready-made dollhouse.

Because the purchase of a dollhouse represents a substantial financial investment, it is best to shop around before you buy. Most miniatures shows include several exhibitors who sell dollhouses. Look at what's available, chat with the builders and discuss custom building and its costs. Visit a local miniatures shop or craft store. Read miniatures publications, checking the advertisements for dollhouse builders and dealers. In time you will have a clear picture of what is available within your price range and be able to make a wise decision in purchasing your dollhouse.

1

2

3

A three-story Federal dollhouse is set off with dormers, shutters and double front steps (1). Such a gingham-papered bedroom takes care to complete (2). Veranda doors can open up the outside to a richly decorated house (3). Electrification has become so simplified, even a person inexperienced with wiring can do it (4).

4

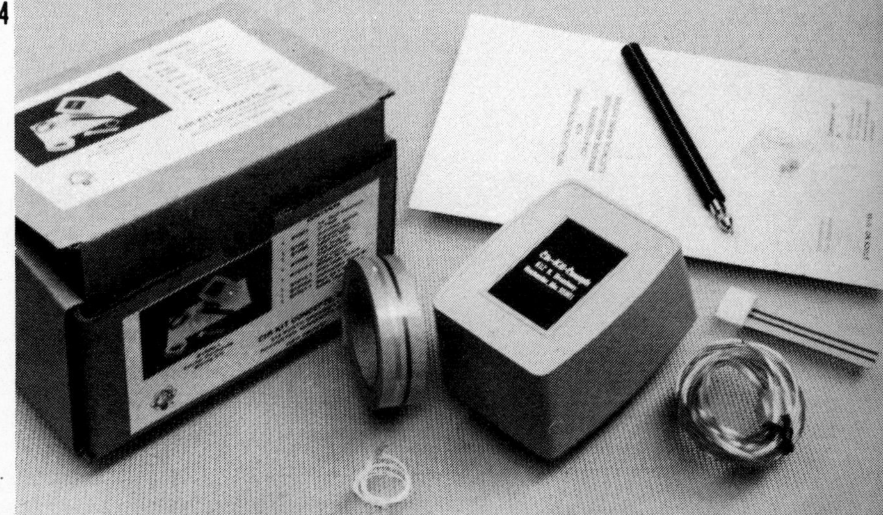

Decorating. Whether bought or built, your dollhouse will one day stand waiting to be decorated and furnished, to become a microcosm of the domestic life of this or an earlier (or future) time. Through the use of lights, furniture and fabrics down to the very dinner on the dining room table, your house will express the tastes of its imaginary inhabitants.

If you feel clumsy at first, your continuing involvement will put you at ease. If you become dissatisfied with the rooms that you decorated earlier and feel compelled to redo them, don't worry. The miniaturists' satisfaction is in the doing, not necessarily in its completion. Like a full-scale house, a dollhouse has an individual evolution. As your likes and dislikes change, so will your feel for the house. However full a dollhouse appears, it is never really finished, and that is the secret of the hobby's hold. It is an ongoing delight.

"Home Improvements." The interior of a dollhouse can so captivate the attention of its owner and those who view it that the outside can be totally ignored. Some dollhouses may appear to have no exterior whatsoever. One may be constructed like a bookshelf, another pushed against a wall so that the front is never seen. But without consideration of the dollhouse as a whole, inside and out, you merely have a collection of decorated rooms.

The truth is, most people find decorating the outside boring compared to the fascinations of finishing and furnishing the inside. Most miniaturists rush through or slight the exterior in their haste to get to the more enticing work. But the outside can be equally engrossing if you consider the beautiful exteriors produced by some of today's outstanding dollhouse builders.

You can fully customize your dollhouse using a wide variety of miniature architectural components. For instance, a dollhouse that comes complete with a plain plywood roof need not remain that way. You can purchase genuine or simulated asphalt tiles, sheets of simulated tiles or genuine cedar shakes, all of which improve a nondescript, unrealistic roof. If you are unhappy with the windows, try replacing them with new moveable ones with perfectly scaled moldings. And if, for instance, you wish to add a brick facade to the front of your dollhouse, you have several options. You can buy perfectly scaled, genuine brick and do your own bricklaying (using "mini mortar"), or you can purchase simulated and textured brick facings that come in thin sheets. (Patterns are also available in flagstone and fieldstone, opening up possibilities for patios, fireplaces, chimneys, walls and other indoor and outdoor masonry details.) There is also clapboard siding available in sheets or in individual planks and, for an English Tudor house, special "stucco" finishes and dark stained miniature beams. Most of these details can be added with the help of white craft glue and will go a long way to transforming an ordinary dollhouse into one of distinction.

Some people are naturally "house conscious." They regard architecture as an art form and look at houses the way others look at paintings. The best way to raise

1

your own architectural awareness is simply to open your eyes. Drive around and look at various houses, noting those that appeal to you. Consider the human drama: the residents' personalities, their economic status and the history of the house. And remember, there are no heating bills, no upkeep costs and no real estate taxes, so reach for just what you want . . . Cape Cod, Victorian, English Tudor or the most modern.

Take a camera with you and shoot pictures of all the houses you like. When the pictures are developed you may find that one design stands out as a favorite. All you need to do then is to find the ready-made dollhouse or kit that most closely matches it. You might also think about having a craftsperson custom build the house for you, or do it yourself.

Like most aspects of miniatures, customizing the outside can become quite addictive once you get into it. If you raise your house consciousness before you purchase or begin building your first dollhouse, you will probably be happier with it in the long run. Many of the extra touches that make a dollhouse special are possible if you are willing to exert some effort and invest a little extra money. It is well worth it.

Landscaping. Once you have customized the outside of your house, you may find it distressing to see your creation sitting in such a stark landscape as a bare table top. Without some greenery, the illusion of life is lost. By mounting the house on a piece of plywood, an area around it is available for landscaping

2

3

Lighting makes more of miniatures (1). Windows are part of a house's character (2). Add a greenhouse to the "grounds" (3).

and "putting in a garden." And by adding trees, plants, grass and even lawn furniture, window boxes, trellises, walls, fences, garden tools, flower pots and other items, you make your house a home.

Before going to artificial sources of greenery, investigate some of the ways in which you can use growing plants around your dollhouse. Many miniaturists find air fern especially versatile. It requires neither food nor water but, as its name implies, lives on air. It is fine and delicate, making it ideal for tiny planters and flower pots or for border plantings around a miniature garden. Air fern can be obtained in florist shops and by mail.

Dried plants can also serve as miniature greenery. One of the most realistic, though leafless, miniature trees can be made from a piece of tumbleweed. In areas where tumbleweed is nonexistent, you may find other plant life which lends itself to representative trees and shrubbery. Keep your eyes open for interesting weeds the next time you take a walk. Dried plants you can buy include the little star flower available in nurseries and flower shops. They are perfect representations of asters or chrysanthemums and come in bright, lively colors.

To copy living plants in miniature and to come up with something realistic is sometimes a bit tricky, but artificial flowers made from either bread dough or clay, when well done can be used extensively, indoors and out.

Model railroading, a cousin to the miniatures hobby, is also a good source for landscaping materials. Although the HO and N scales are far smaller than the one-twelfth scale of dollhouse miniatures, many of the materials are easily adaptable. For example, an artificial plant meant to represent a large tree in HO scale can be a small one in your miniature garden. Trim the trunk of the tree, reshape its branches and it becomes a one-twelfth scale bush.

Surround your house with lawn and paths for a welcoming look. There is an artificial "green lawn" that model railroaders use that can be cut and glued right onto your plywood base. For contour, put down a base of Celluclay instant papier mâché or a special model railroading landscape mix. After it has dried it can be painted in appropriate shades of green and brown to represent lawn and garden areas. And lay gravel, also available at model railroad shops, to form garden paths.

Like every aspect of your dollhouse, the landscaping will require some planning. Fashions in gardens come and go just as they do in interior decorating. Make sure that yours is in keeping with the period and style of your house. While a formal garden may be appropriate for an English Tudor house, it would be out of place beside a 1920s farmhouse. A little research in history and gardening books will keep you on the right track.

As small as they are, miniatures require an investment—of time, energy and some money. The return is seeing the room or dollhouse come to life.

Sources

Organizations

AT THE BEGINNING of your involvement in miniatures, you might prefer to work alone developing and crafting the tiny tables, chairs and other pieces with which to fill your room or dollhouse. But, eventually you will seek out other craftspeople to share tales and techniques or just to enjoy the pleasure of the company of those involved in the "little" world. The following organizations are your link to other miniaturists. Of course, there are many local miniatures organizations, some affiliated with N.A.M.E. and some not. Check with N.A.M.E. for the address of a chapter near you and with your neighborhood miniatures or crafts shop for the names of other individuals who might be organized or interested in organizing a formal or informal group.

National Association of Miniature Enthusiasts (N.A.M.E.)
1309 W. Valencia
Suite H
Fullerton, CA 92633

A national organization with regional clubs throughout the country, N.A.M.E. fosters the enjoyment of miniatures, sponsors shows and propagates information through its publication, *Miniature Gazette,* a subscription to which is included in each membership. The organization's activities include every aspect of the miniatures hobby, from collecting to crafting, although the general orientation seems to be toward the collector. Both individual and group memberships are available. Write for free information.

Publications

In Miniatures we have opened the door and sketched a panorama of the world of miniatures for you. The following magazines and books can take you still further.

Periodicals

Dollhouse & Miniature News
3 Orchard Lane
Kirkwood, MO 63122

Edited and published by former newspaper woman and well-known miniaturist, Marian O'Brien, this newsletter appears ten times a year. It offers chitchat and news about the world of miniatures, opinion, some how-to articles and personality profiles. $10.00 per year.

Miniature Collector
170 Fifth Ave.
New York, NY 10010

As its name suggests, this magazine is edited primarily for the collector of miniatures. Feature articles include in-depth looks at individual craftspeople and their work along with extensive show reports, complete with full-color pictures of the outstanding items exhibited. Single copy price, $2.50; subscription, $12.00 per year. Published bi-monthly.

Miniatures Dealer
Boynton & Associates
Clifton House
Clifton, VA 22024

Anyone seriously considering entering the miniatures business, either as a craftsperson or as a retailer, should read this magazine to keep abreast of trends and developments within the industry.

The Miniature Magazine
P.O. Box 700
Newton, NJ 07860

Originally introduced in 1976 as an annual publication, this magazine is a spin-off of *Creative Crafts,* a general crafts magazine that has long given extensive coverage to miniatures. Now published quarterly, its format includes every aspect of miniatures, with emphasis on crafts and how-to articles frequently written by well-known miniaturists. Events, product news and reviews and columns dealing with specific areas of interest such as historical reproduction and ceramics are part of the editorial package. Single copy price, $1.50; subscription, $6.00 per year.

Nutshell News
1035 Newkirk Drive
LaJolla, CA 92037

The oldest of all the miniature publications, this one has as friendly and enthusiastic an air as one could hope to find in a magazine dealing with a hobby noted for its charm and warmth. Neither strictly for the craftsperson nor for the collector, *Nutshell News'* goal seems to be that of orienting the miniature enthusiast to the world of miniatures. Single copy price, $2.50; subscription, $12.00 per year. Published bi-monthly.

The Scale Cabinetmaker
Dorsett Miniatures, Inc.
P.O. Box 87
Pembroke, VA 24136

Describing itself as "A Journal for the Miniaturist," *The Scale Cabinetmaker* is devoted entirely to the interests of the fine-miniatures craftsperson. Its approach to the making of scale miniatures is serious and intelligent. All material is thoroughly researched and of top quality. Plans, tips, sources and detailed step-by-step instructions are included in each issue. Single copy price, $3.75; subscription, $12.00 per year. Quarterly.

Books

The Book of Miniatures: Furniture & Accessories by Helen Ruthberg. Written by a fine artist-turned-miniaturist, *The Book of Miniatures* is a treasury of ideas, patterns and techniques, most of which use simple, inexpensive materials. Unlike many miniaturists who work in improvised materials, Ruthberg creates miniature settings that are exquisitely detailed and perfectly scaled. Her book suggests hundreds of ways in which you can use your imagination to furnish miniature settings. The emphasis is upon accessories, although there is also a sizable section devoted to furniture construction. (Chilton Book Company, Radnor, PA 19089; hardcover, $13.95; softcover, $7.95.)

The Collector's Guide to Dollhouses and Dollhouse Miniatures by Marian Maeve O'Brien. A comprehensive and lavishly illustrated book written by a veteran miniatures collector, *The Collector's Guide* provides a close look at some of the outstanding miniature collections and offers the would-be collector some guidelines on how to begin. Especially helpful is an extensive list of craftspeople and their products. This book will prove extremely valuable to the hobbyist who intends to concentrate primarily upon collecting and wishes to explore the various directions possible within this aspect of miniatures. Illustrated with many black and white photographs and a full-color section, it includes both antique and contemporary miniature collections. (Hawthorne Books, Inc., 260 Madison Ave., New York, NY 10016; hardcover, $16.95; softcover, $8.95.)

The Complete Book of Making Miniatures by Thelma Newman and Virginia Merrill. The result of a collaboration between a master miniature craftsperson and an outstanding crafts author, this book is authoritative and complete. It draws heavily upon the work of other craftspeople, showing some of the best that is being produced today. Many techniques are presented with step-by-step photos and clearly written instructions. Newman's full-size craft specialty in plastic gives this book some treatments and techniques not usually found in miniature work. (Crown Publishers, Inc., One Park Ave., New York, NY 10016; hardcover, $12.95; softcover, $6.95.)

Inside the World of Miniatures & Dollhouses by Bernard Rosner and Jay Beckerman. Whether your bent is toward crafting or collecting, this book is your door to "inside" miniatures. It is the first book to acknowledge the existence of a miniatures industry and to offer sources for miniature furniture kits, dollhouse components, tools and other materials required by the miniature crafts hobbyist. Comprehensive in its scope, it gives coverage to the work of individual craftspeople and manufacturers and includes information on miniature antiques. The book also contains complete details and plans for constructing both a miniature room and an entire Williamsburg Colonial dollhouse. (David McKay Co., Inc., Two Park Ave., New York, NY 10016; hardcover, $17.95; softcover, $8.95.)

Make Your Own Dollhouses and Dollhouse Miniatures by Marian Maeve O'Brien. This is a large and comprehensive book aimed at the miniatures craftsperson who wishes to build and furnish a dollhouse. Full of patterns, tips and construction techniques, it contains many unusual items which the author has contrived herself. Chapters are devoted to general dollhouse building and the use of specific crafts in miniature making, including the metal, paper and bead crafts. (Hawthorne Books, Inc., 260 Madison Ave., New York, NY 10016; hardcover, $16.95; softcover, $8.95.)

Miniature Room Settings by Helen Ruthberg. Ruthberg's specialty is the "theme room," the miniature room which has been constructed around a single idea. In this book, she explores the many opportunities for creative expression that are presented by the single miniature room. Complete directions are given for planning and constructing the room, plus detailed instructions for seven different settings of the author's own design. A final section of the book is devoted to the miniature rooms of other craftspeople. (Chilton Book Company, Radnor, PA 19089; hardcover, $12.50; softcover, $7.95.)

Needlework in Miniature by Virginia Merrill and Jean Jessop. *Needlework* presents techniques and inspiration for making miniature rugs, upholstery, bedspreads and many other dollhouse items. Many needlepoint projects are presented with charts and well illustrated instructions. The work of the best needle artists is shown extensively. Scale and fine detail are emphasized throughout the book. (Crown Publishers, Inc., One Park Ave., New York, NY 10016; hardcover, $10.95; softcover, $6.95.)

Manufacturers

As small as miniatures are, they still can't be created out of thin air; you must either make them yourself or rely on a dealer or manufacturer to supply you with the parts and pieces you need. We have chosen not to list the enumerable miniatures distributors across the country but, instead, suggest that you check your local telephone book listings under "Miniatures," "Crafts" and "Hobbies" for the miniatures shop nearest you.

If the local shop doesn't carry the materials or pieces you want, then you must turn to a manufacturer directly. Here, we have listed miniatures manufacturers according to specialties. A few you will find included more than once which indicates the diversification of some manufacturers.

Ask those manufacturers whose wares you favor to supply you with a catalog of their line. But remember: some are solo operations so a reply may take time. Miniatures is a big and busy world.

ACCESSORIES

Clare Bell Brass Works
Queen St.
P.O. Box 369
Southington, CT 06489
(metal accessories)

Creative World Miniatures
39 Westmoreland Ave.
White Plains, NY 10606
(collectors' plates and framed prints)

Diana, Inc.
2685 W. Coyle
Elk Grove, IL 60007
(assorted accessories)

Glass Concepts Co.
1424 Buena Vista Dr.
Wheaton, IL 60187
(miniature glassware)

Grandmother Stover's, Inc.
1331 King Ave.
Columbus, OH 43212
(assorted accessories)

Jacqu*Min, Inc.
7601 Forsyth Blvd.
St. Louis, MO 63105
(assorted accessories)

The Keshishian Collection
Box 3002
San Clemente, CA 92672
(miniature oriental rugs)

Vico Mfg.
P.O. Box 1508
Atlantic City, NJ 08404
(pewter miniatures)

Wonderland Originals, Ltd.
144 Lemon St.
P.O. Box 1555
Reading, PA 19603
(solid brass miniatures)

Yum Yums, Inc.
14741 Oxnard St.
Van Nuys, CA 91411
(miniature food and other accessories)

DOLLHOUSES

American Miniatures
102 Second Ave. N.
Mt. Vernon, IA 52314
(kits)

AMSI Miniatures
115-B Bellam Blvd.
P.O. Box 3497
San Rafael, CA 94902
(components and plans)

Batrie Corp.
19 Rear Stone St.
Walpole, MA 02081
(kits and supplies)

Carlson's Miniatures, Inc.
Rt. 1, Box 306
Delavan, WI 53115
(kits and houses, components)

Doll Domiciles
P.O. Box 91026
Atlanta, GA 30344
(plans and accessories)

Dollhouse Factory
1045 Merrill St.
Menlo Park, CA 94025
(building materials, kits and plans)

The Dollhouse Factory
Box 456
157 Main St.
Lebanon, NJ 08833
(readymade and custom houses, supplies)

Mischen Manufacturing Co.
32 Half Moon Dr.
El Paso, TX 79915
(dollhouses)

Plaid Enterprises, Inc.
6553 Warren Dr.
P.O. Drawer E
Norcross, GA 30091
(complete building systems)

Real Good Toys
Box 706
Montpelier, VT 05602
(modular add-on dollhouses; tongue-in-groove construction)

Woodline Products
245 E. Adele
Villa Park, IL 60181
(kits)

ELECTRICAL SYSTEMS AND LIGHTING FIXTURES

Chrysolite, Inc.
5118 Midfield Dr.
Portage, MI 49081

Cir-Kit Concepts, Inc.
612 N. Broadway
Rochester, MN 55901

Elect-a-Lite
742-B E. Arctic Ave.
Santa Maria, CA 93454

Illinois Hobbycraft Inc.
605 N. Broadway
Aurora, IL 60505

FINISHED FURNITURE

Andrews Miniatures
Patrick & Center Sts.
Ashland, VA 23005

B. Shackman & Company
85 Fifth Ave.
New York, NY 10003

Collector Miniatures, Inc.
R.D. 1
Quakertown, PA 18951

The George Spencer Collection
1325 Marsten Rd.
Burlingame, CA 94010

Goebel Miniatures & Co.
105 White Plains Rd.
Tarrytown, NY 10591

Jacu*Min, Inc.
7601 Forsyth Blvd.
St. Louis, MO 63105

New England Miniature Furniture Co.
Daniels Village
Dayville, CT 06241

Reminiscence
3206 Old Coach Dr.
Camarillo, CA 93010

Sonia Messer Co., Inc.
4115 San Fernando Rd.
Glendale, CA 91204

FINISHING MATERIALS

J. Hermes
Box 4023
El Monte, CA 91734
(wallpapers)

Midwest Products Co.
400 S. Indiana St.
Hobart, IN 46342
(wood trimming, flooring)

Mini-Brick & Stone Co.
343 Route 46
Fairfield, NJ 07006
(flooring, slate, bricks, roof shingles, mortar)

Mini Graphics
1331 Stonemill Court
Cincinnati, OH 45215
(wallpaper, fabric, carpeting)

Northeastern Scale Models, Inc.
Box 425
Methuen, MA 01844
(wood strips, moldings, siding materials)

Somerset Lumber and Hardware Co.
Forest Wood Products Div.
1022 Hamilton St.
Somerset, NJ 08873
(miniature asphalt, granular asphalt, slate roofing, shingles)

S/W Crafts, Inc.
600 Western Ave.
Lombard, IL 60148
(textured brick paneling)

FURNITURE KITS

B & B Miniatures
13110 70th Ave.
Coal Valley, IL 61240

Chrysnbon, Inc.
4628 Wolf Rd.
Western Springs, IL 60558

Perfection Products Co.
P.O. Box 6871
Greensboro, NC 27405

Scientific Models, Inc.
340 Snyder Ave.
Berkeley Heights, NJ 07901

X-Acto
45-35 Van Dam St.
Long Island City, NY 11101

KITS & MATERIALS

Connoisseur Studio, Inc.
P.O. Box 7187
Louisville, KY 40207
(air drying clay)

Doreen Sinnett Designs, Inc.
P.O. Box 2055
Newport Beach, CA 92663
(materials and kits for making miniature rugs)

Duncan Arts & Crafts
5673 E. Shields
Fresno, CA 93727
(ceramics, molds and materials)

Needlepunch
1409 Fifth St.
Berkeley, CA 94710
(materials and tools for hooked rugs)

Plaid Enterprises, Inc.
6553 Warren Dr.
P.O. Drawer E
Norcross, GA 30091
(paints and craft supplies)

Polyform Products Co.
9420 W. Byron St.
Schiller Park, IL 60176
(oven baking clay)

Teka Fine Line Brushes, Inc.
3704 Bedford Ave.
Brooklyn, NY 11229

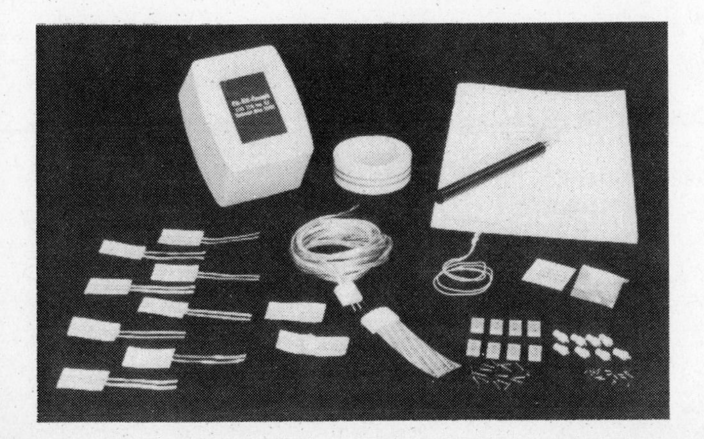

Westwood Ceramic Supply Co.
14400 Lomitas Ave.
City of Industry, CA 91746
(home oven clay)

The Whimsey
13110 70th Ave.
Coal Valley, IL 61240
(curtain pleater)

LANDSCAPING AND FLORAL SUPPLIES

Life-Like Products Corp.
1600 Union Ave.
Baltimore, MD 21211
(landscaping materials)

Posy Patch Originals
P.O. Box 38123
Atlanta, GA 30334
(miniature plants, flowers and gardening supplies)

LARGE MAIL-ORDER SUPPLY HOUSES

The Doll House, Inc.
375 Pharr Rd., NE
Suite 117
Atlanta, GA 30305
(catalog, $3.00)

AMSI Miniatures
115-B Bellam Blvd.
P.O. Box 3497
San Rafael, CA 94902
(catalog, $3.50)

Angela's Dollhouse, Inc.
P.O. Box 84
Pelham, NY 10803
(catalog, $3.00)

TOOLS, HAND

X-Acto
45-35 Van Dam St.
Long Island City, NY 11101
(knives, saw, mitre boxes and clamps)

TOOLS, POWER

Dremel Mfg. Company
Div. Emerson Electric Co.
4915 21st St.
Racine, WI 53406
(Moto-tool, Moto-Shop, Moto-Lathe)

Jarmac, Inc.
P.O. Box 2785
Springfield, IL 62708
(miniatures table saw and disc sander)

SOURCES AND CRAFTSPEOPLE

The Miniatures Catalog
Clifton House
Clifton, VA 22024

Catalog listing over 400 manufacturers and craftspeople whose products are presently available. A 16-page, full-color section is devoted entirely to museum-quality miniatures. Over 4,000 products are shown, described and priced, all available at dealers or directly from the craftspeople. Suggested retail price for 400-page book, $9.95. If your local miniature, craft or hobby shop does not carry it, the catalog can be ordered directly from the publisher for $10.95. (Make check or money order payable to *The Miniatures Catalog*.)

Displays

To stimulate your interest and incentive and to provide an example of perfection in miniatures work, there are a number of excellent miniatures displays you can visit. The following 14 museums are the most well-known and contain the most exemplary miniature work in the U.S. and Canada.

Arizona

Phoenix Art Museum
Phoenix, AZ
(permanent exhibit of 16 Thorne rooms)

California

Mott Miniatures
Knott's Berry Farm
Buena Park, CA
(largest display of miniatures anywhere)

Canada

Miniature World
635 Humboldt St.
Victoria, B.C.

District of Columbia

Smithsonian Institution
Washington, D. C.
(Faith Bradford dollhouse)

Washington Doll's House & Toy Museum
5234 44th St.
Washington, D.C.

Illinois

Art Institute of Chicago
Adams and Michigan Ave.
Chicago, IL
(Thorne rooms)

Museum of Science and Industry
57th St. and Lakeshore Dr.
Chicago, IL
(Colleen Moore dollhouse)

Kentucky

Gallery of Miniatures
317 Seay St.
Glasgow, KY

Massachusetts

Essex Institute
Salem, MA
(1852 Warren House)

Sturbridge Village
Brimfield Turnpike
Sturbridge, MA
(Colonial rooms)

Missouri

Frost Museum of Miniatures
Highway 76
Branson, MO

New York

Margaret Woodbury Strong Museum
700 Allen Creek Rd.
Rochester, NY

Museum of the City of New York
1220 Fifth Ave.
New York, NY

Vermont

Enchanted Doll House Museum
Manchester Center, VT

Miniatures Techniques And Inquiries

ALTHOUGH IT HAS not been within the scope of *Miniatures* to give you a how-to hand-up into the world of miniatures, here are a few techniques to get you started and the answers to several questions that may arise as you delve deeper into this popular hobby. For more and advanced techniques look to one or more of the recommended books in the "Sources" section at the back of this book.

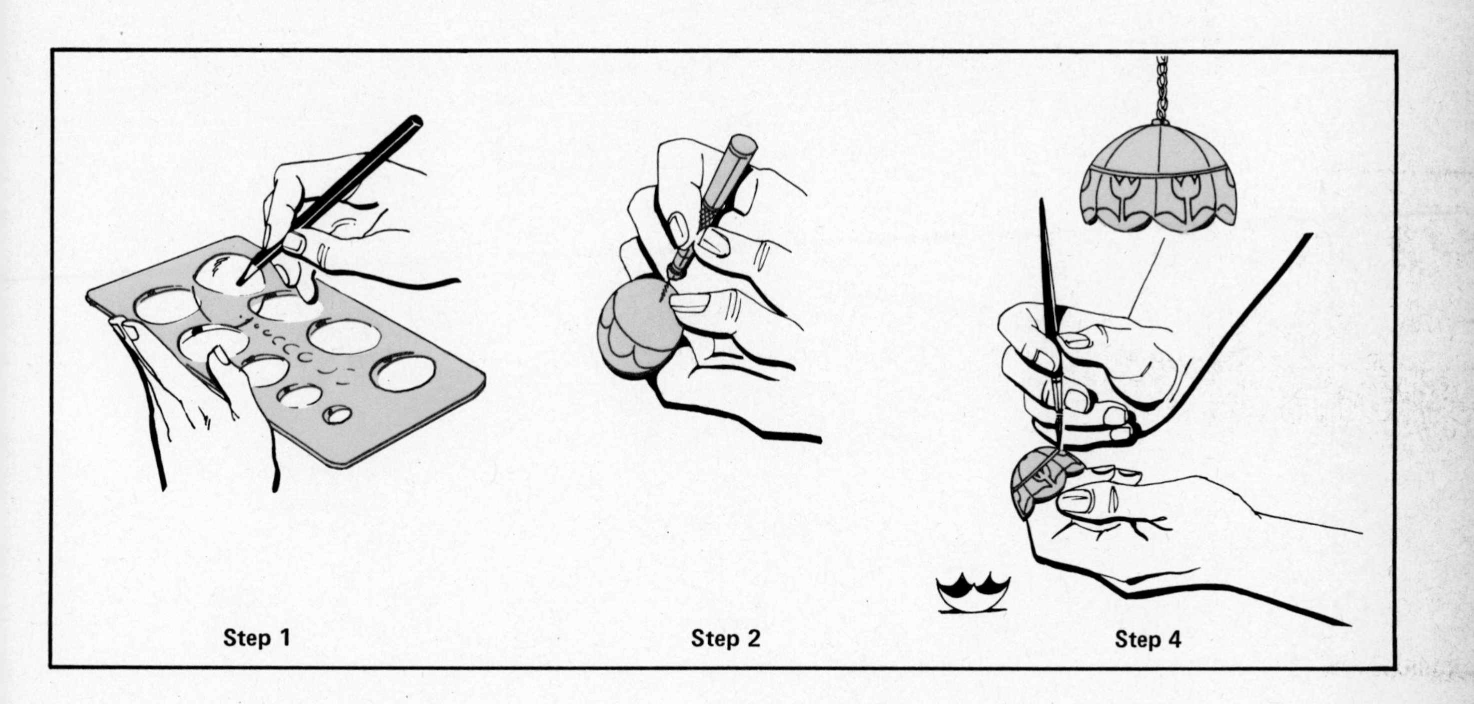

Step 1 Step 2 Step 4

How can I make a "Tiffany" Lamp from a Ping-Pong ball?

1. Hold a template over a white Ping-Pong ball and mark eight segments evenly. (The template should be large enough to allow a quarter of the ball to push through.)
2. Pierce the ball at the top and bottom with a very small hand drill.
3. Divide the ball at the markings and cut scallops around the edge of the larger section with cuticle scissors.
4. Using India ink and bright, translucent acrylic paints, draw and color in your own design. (To simulate the lead lines between pieces of "glass" use black paint.)
5. Wire and hang the lamp over a miniature dining room table or in a dollhouse foyer.

Note: To reproduce a second style, cut points around the edge of the smaller ball section and glue it—pedals up—to the larger lamp "shade." Separate the two sections with a tiny brass ring for authenticity.

Step 1

What's the best way to wallpaper a miniature room?

1. Use wallpaper paste (wheat glue) available in paint or hardware stores; Yes glue, which is hard to find but available in some art supply stores; or Glutoline wallpaper paste with sizing, also in paint stores. (Rubber cements, airplane or hobby glue and white craft glue are not recommended.) Mix to ice cream consistency.

2. Cut a pattern of thin cardboard of the surface to be covered if it is irregular or difficult to get to. Trace pattern onto wallpaper. Cut.

3. Prime (seal) the surface with a flat wall paint, varnish or shellac.

4. Sand down bumps on the wall surface.

5. Apply paste to paper with one-half inch brush.

6. Apply paper to surface and roll out air bubbles or wrinkles with a rubber roller or brayer or press out with wadded toweling.

Hint: Cut the paper into sections and apply piecemeal (matching the pattern) if walls with windows, doors, a fireplace, etc. are to be papered.

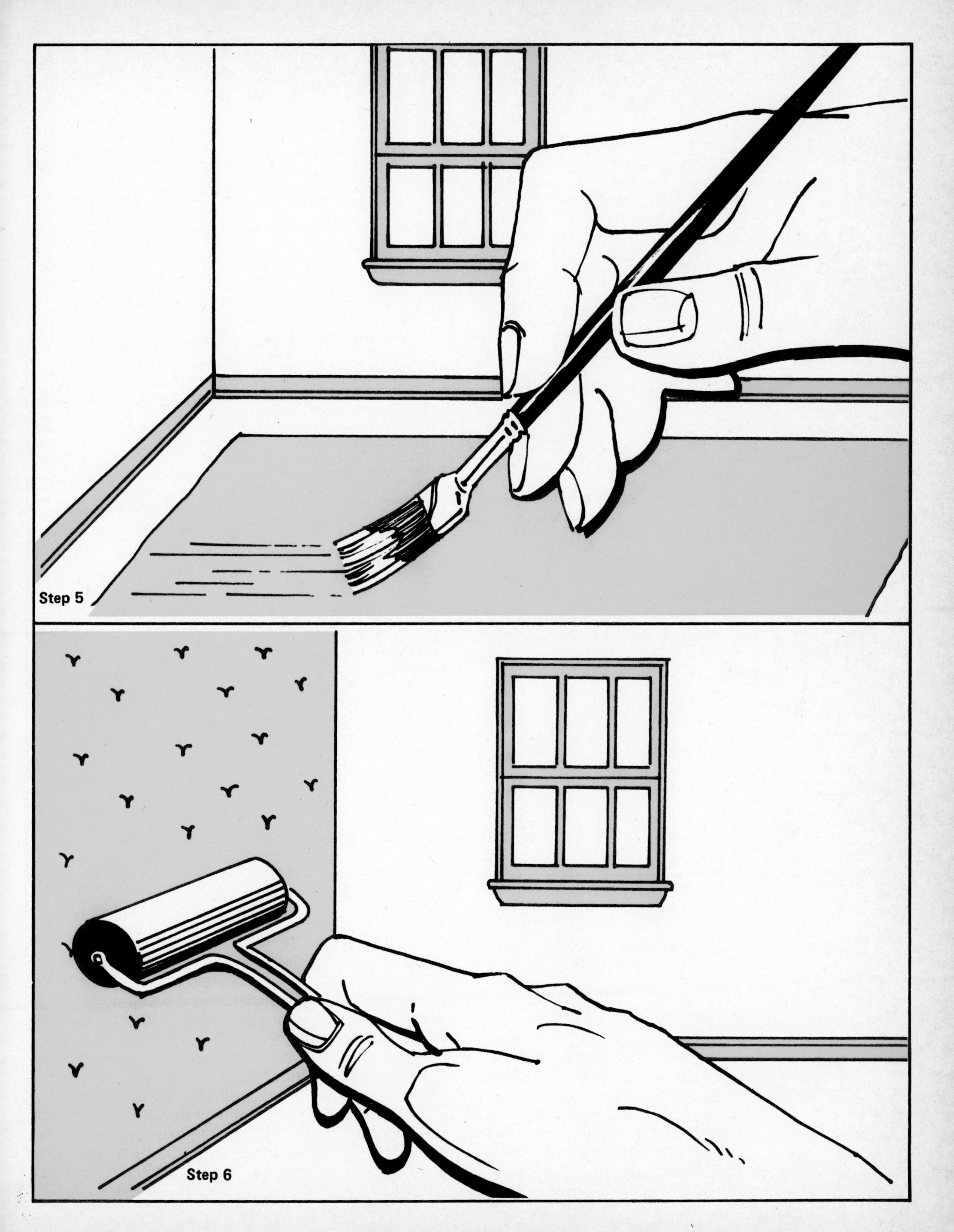
Step 5
Step 6

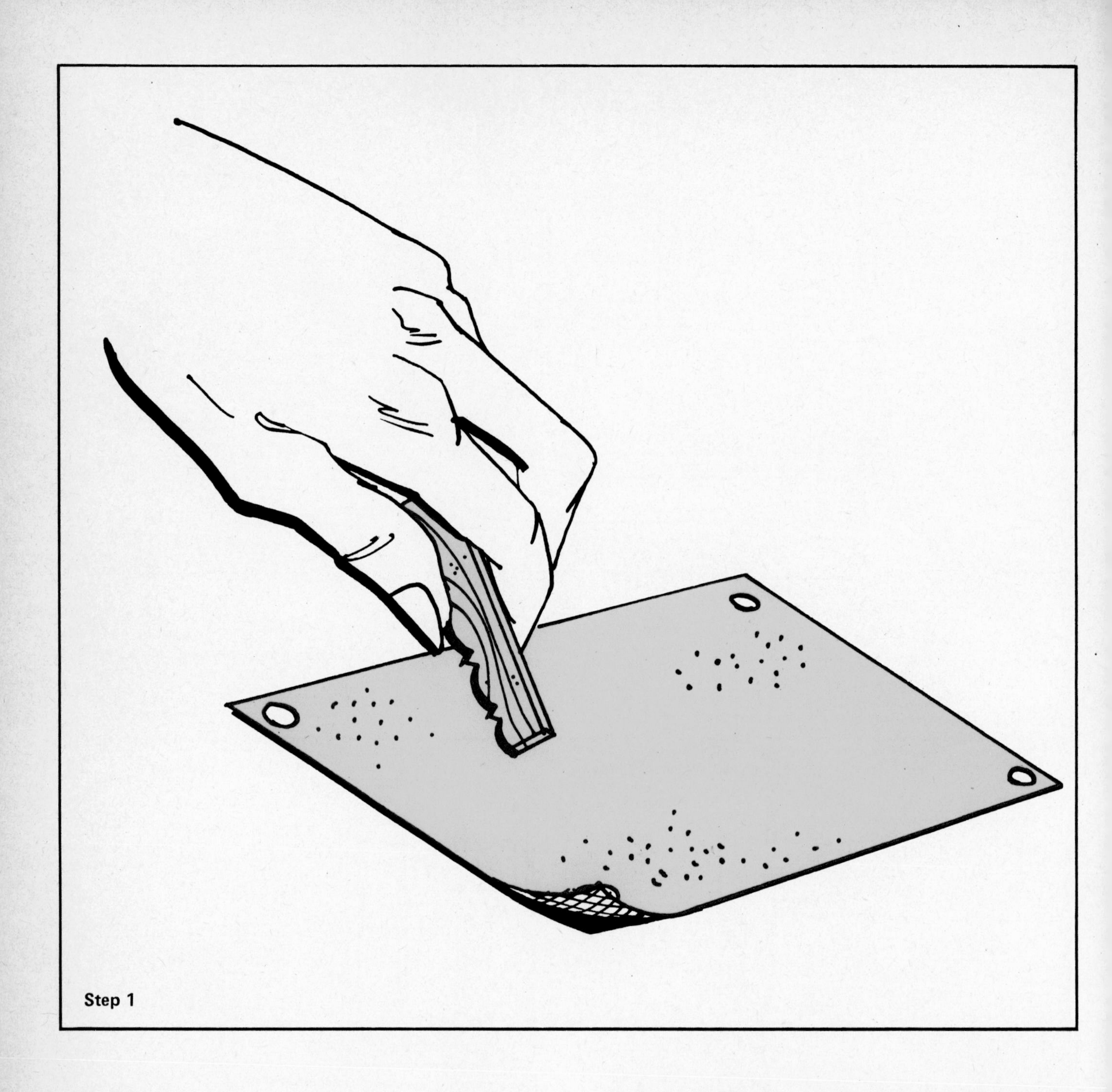

What are the steps in assembling pieces of a miniature furniture kit?

1. Sanding: Use 150, 180 and 220 grit sandpaper, progressively. Tack the sandpaper on a flat surface facing up. Sand the furniture part by rubbing it back and forth on the stationary sandpaper until all scratch marks are removed. (Hold the piece up to the light to check.)

2. Trial assembly: Study the kit drawings. Assemble the parts using rubber bands to hold. Check the fit of all the joints and make any necessary adjustments by resanding carefully.

3. Gluing: Apply a thin film of carpenter's glue to both surfaces of the joint, using a flat toothpick as an applicator. Clamp or press joined pieces with a heavy book. Wipe off excess glue with a damp cotton swab and check for squareness before glue sets. Let glue dry for 30 minutes.

4. Staining: Sand surfaces lightly with a piece of 150 grit or above sandpaper. Scrape off dried glue at edges with a small knife, chisel or other sharp object. Apply oil base stain according to the manufacturer's directions.

5. Finishing: Spray piece lightly with lacquer. Let dry thoroughly four to five hours. Rub down with 0000 steel wool. Repeat process twice more. Wax surface with a good furniture paste wax. Attach hardware.

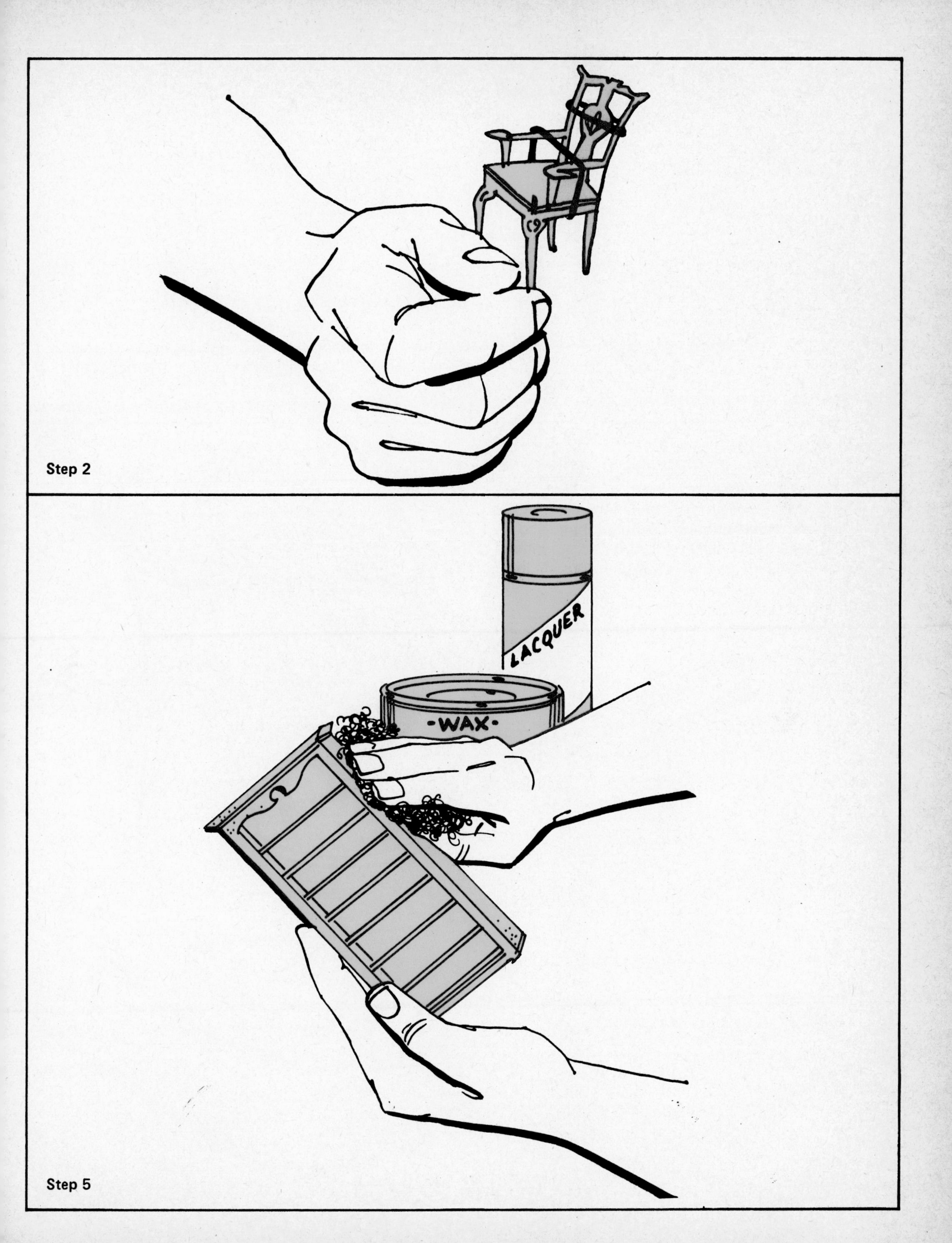
Step 2
LACQUER
-WAX-
Step 5

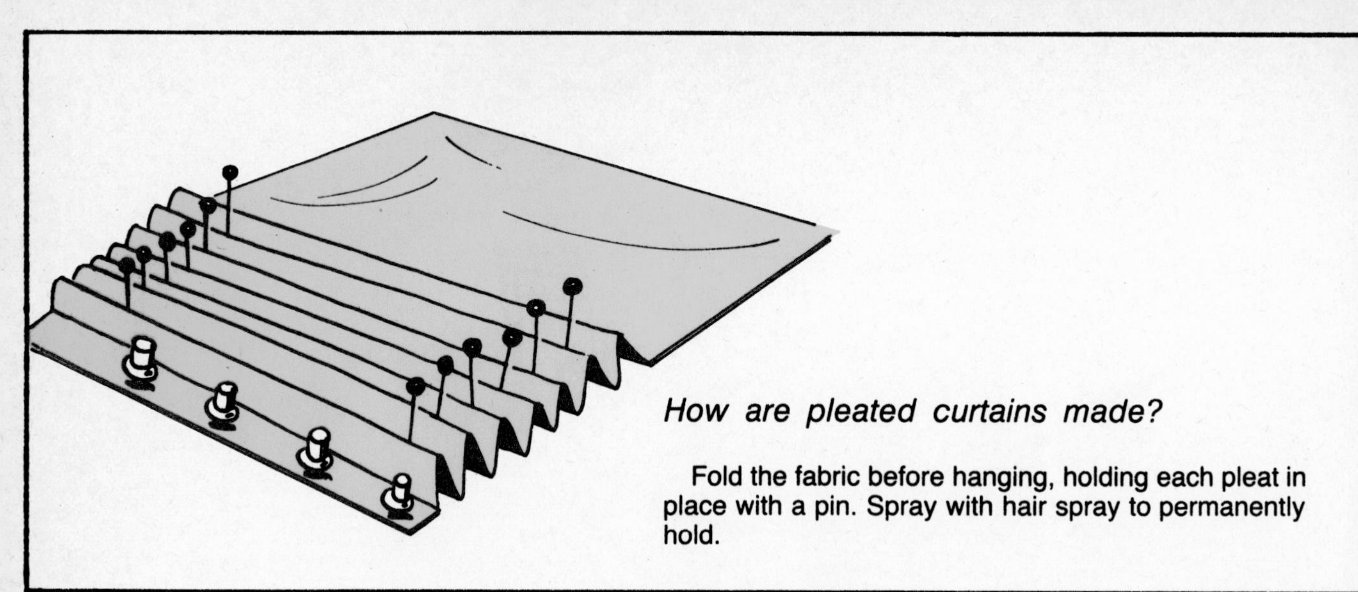

How are pleated curtains made?

Fold the fabric before hanging, holding each pleat in place with a pin. Spray with hair spray to permanently hold.

How would a magnifying glass help in miniatures work?

Dremel Manufacturing Company has recently introduced a large magnifying light on an adjustable stand for needlepoint and other close work. It leaves the hands free.

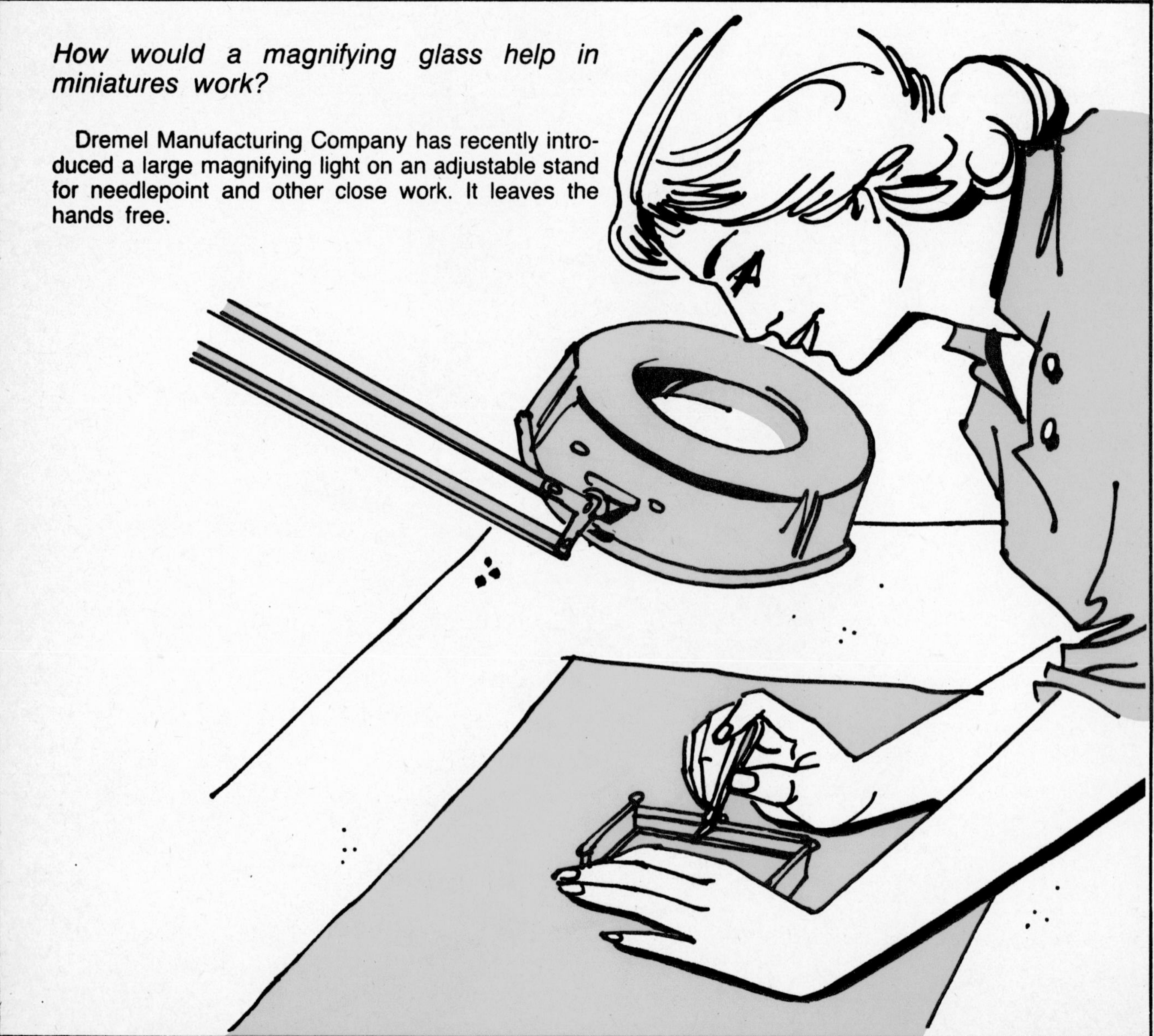

What is the best way to display a dollhouse?

Place the dollhouse in the center of the room or mount it on a lazy susan so that it can be seen from all sides. (Mechanisms for lazy susans are available in do-it-yourself centers.)

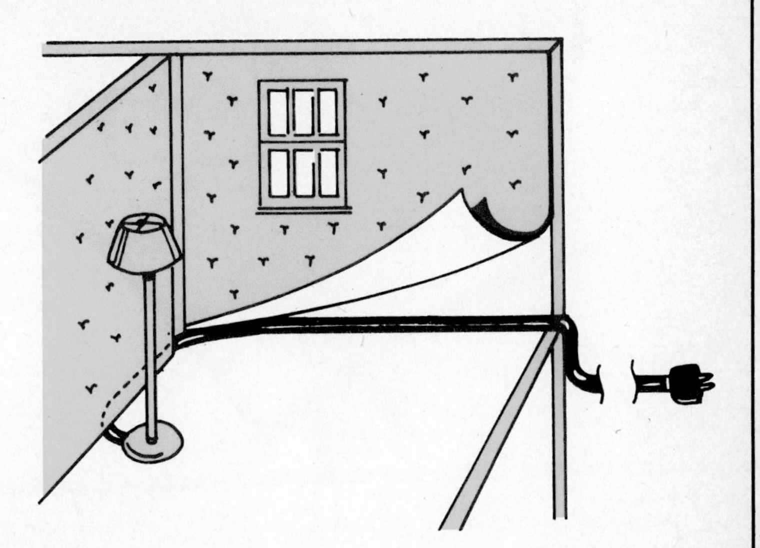

How are electrical wires concealed in a dollhouse?

Place flat wires under moldings or beneath wallpaper, using special electrical tape that has been developed for dollhouse use.

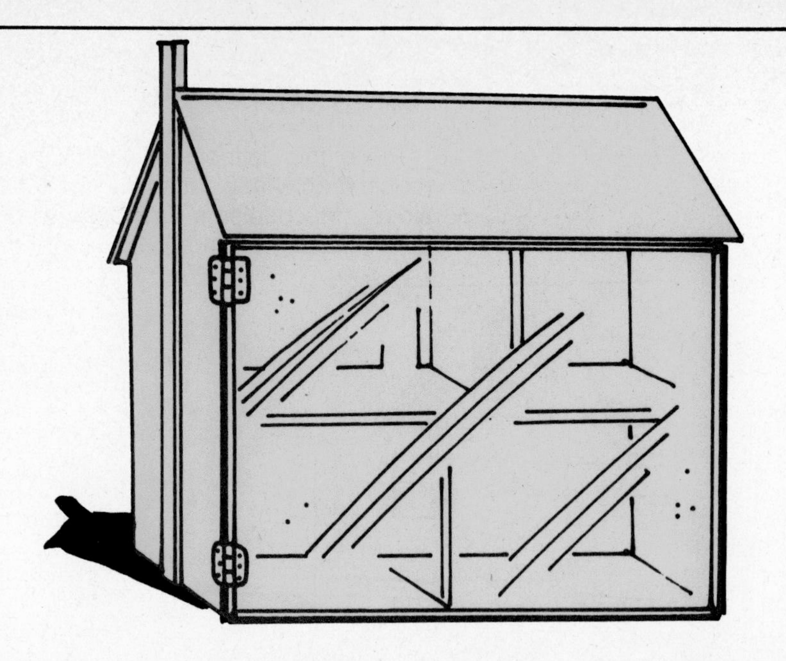

How can I protect my miniatures from dust and fading?

Close up the doll house completely when not in use so that only the exterior is visible. Outfit the open back with an acrylic door cut to size and fitted with molding and hinges, and place the dollhouse where it is not subject to direct sunlight. Smaller miniatures setting can also be protected with acrylic coverings.

Will my homeowner's insurance cover my miniatures collection?

Your homeowner's or tenant's insurance will protect your miniatures collection against fire, theft and other damage but not against a breakage or "mysterious disappearance." Carry a floater on your insurance policy which includes these eventualities. (The rates for this will vary from state to state.)